SIKHISM
WORLD RELIGIONS
3202567

by
Nikky-Guninder Kaur Singh

Facts On File, Inc.

SIKHISM
World Religions

Copyright © 1993 by Nikky-Guninder Kaur Singh

Facts On File, Inc.
11 Penn Plaza
New York NY 10001

Library of Congress Cataloging-in-Publication Data
Singh, Nikky-Guninder Kaur.
  Sikhism / by Nikky-Guninder Kaur Singh.
    p. cm. — (World religions)
  Includes bibliographical references and index.
  Summary: Discusses the origin of Sikhism as an attempt to reconcile the beliefs of Muslims and Hindus, the conflicts it has faced over the centuries, and recent developments.
    ISBN 0-8160-2446-4 (alk. paper)
    1. Sikhism—Juvenile literature. [1. Sikhism.] I. Series.
  BL2018.S5175   1993
  294.6—dc20   92-33179

Facts On File books are available at special discounts when purchased in bulk quantities for businesses, associations, institutions, or sales promotions. Please call our Special Sales Department in New York at 212/967-8800 or 800/322-8755.

You can find Facts On File on the World Wide Web at http://www.factsonfile.com

Developed by Brown Publishing Network, Inc. Design Production by Jennifer Angell/Brown Publishing Network, Inc. Photo Research by Nina Whitney.

Photo credits:
Cover: Sikh Sardar with the Biwan Sikh School, circa 1840. (The Bridgeman Art Library, London). *Title page*: A Sikh worshiper at prayer at the Bangla Sahib temple at Delhi, India. Bonnie Kamin. *Table of Contents page*: Harimandir, or the Golden Temple in Amritsar, India. The Bettmann Archive. *Pages 6–7* Cameramann Int'l.; *9* Jai Singh Khalsa; *11* Bonnie Kamin; *16–17* Christine Osborne (Middle East Pictures); *22* Jai Singh Khalsa; *25* Bonnie Kamin; *28* Christine Osborne (Middle East Pictures); *30–31* Religious News Service; *35* The Bettmann Archives; *39* Christine Osborne (Middle East Pictures); *42* Christine Osborne (Middle East Pictures); *44* Christine Osborne (Middle East Pictures); *46–47* Christine Osborne (Middle East Pictures); *51* Nikky-Guninder Kaur Singh; *54* Christine Osborne (Middle East Pictures); *56–57* Christine Osborne (Middle East Pictures); *59* Arvind Garg; *62* Christine Osborne (Middle East Pictures); *64–65* Christine Osborne (Middle East Pictures); *66* Christine Osborne (Middle East Pictures); *68* Nikky-Guninder Kaur Singh; *73* Christine Osborne (Middle East Pictures); *74* Christine Osborne (Middle East Pictures); *76* Christine Osborne (Middle East Pictures); *86–87* Christine Osborne (Middle East Pictures); *89* Jai Singh Khalsa; *90* Christine Osborne (Middle East Pictures); *93* Arvind Garg; *97* The Bettmann Archive; *102* Savitri Khalsa; *104–105* Christine Osborne (Middle East Pictures); *107* Christine Osborne (Middle East Pictures); *111* Savitri Khalsa; *112–113* Savitri Khalsa; *115* Christine Osborne (Middle East Pictures); *119* The Bettmann Archive; *120* Christine Osborne (Middle East Pictures).

Printed in the United States of America
RRD PKG 10 9 8 7 6 5 4
This book is printed on acid-free paper.

TABLE OF CONTENTS

Preface

The 20th century is sometimes called a "secular age," meaning, in effect, that religion is not an especially important issue for most people. But there is much evidence to suggest that this is not true. In many societies, including the United States, religion and religious values shape the lives of millions of individuals and play a key role in politics and culture as well.

The World Religions series, of which this book is a part, is designed to appeal to both students and general readers. The books offer clear, accessible overviews of the major religious traditions and institutions of our time. Each volume in the series describes where a particular religion is practiced, its origins and history, its central beliefs and important rituals, and its contributions to world civilization. Carefully chosen photographs complement the text, and a glossary and bibliography are included to help readers gain a more complete understanding of the subject at hand.

Religious institutions and spirituality have always played a central role in world history. These books will help clarify what religion is all about and reveal both the similarities and differences in the great spiritual traditions practiced around the world today.

Area where Sikhism is a major influence

CHAPTER 1

Introduction: Sikhism and the Modern World

The Sikh religion is the youngest of all world religions. It began about five hundred years ago in the Punjab region of India. Most of its followers still live in this fertile region, which is located in the foothills of the Himalaya Mountains in northwest India.

In all, there are about sixteen million Sikhs in the world today. About ten million of them live in the Punjab; the rest have spread to other parts of India and beyond. There are Sikh populations in Britian, the United States, Canada, East Africa, the Arab Emirates, Iran, Malaysia, and Hong Kong.

Although Sikhs represent only about two percent of India's huge population, they are highly visible. What makes them dominant in society is their strong work ethic, which is part of their religion, and their courageousness. A large proportion of India's military officers are Sikhs, as are many of its army troops and many of its airline pilots. Sikhs are also known to be fine athletes, and many have represented India on Olympic teams.

Sikhs may be found in cities and towns the world over, where they have settled in search of work and education. In most

metropolitan areas, one can find Sikh professors and doctors, taxi drivers and shopkeepers, students, mechanics, and office workers. During the race between the United States and the former Soviet Union to put the first person on the moon, Sikhs in their far-flung communities joked that whoever reached the moon first would find a Sikh already there.

It is fairly easy to recognize a traditional Sikh. Every Sikh man's surname is *Singh,* meaning "lion" or "lion-hearted." Every Sikh woman's surname is *Kaur,* meaning "princess." Both men and women wear a steel bracelet around the right wrist as an emblem of their faith. Sikh men can often be identified by their beards and by the turban, a headdress that consists of a long length of colorful cloth wrapped around the head. The turban is the most notable feature of Sikh men's clothing. Other men of India may wear the turban, often a feature of Muslim dress, but it is particularly associated with Sikhs, who wear it as a religious symbol. Such a visible symbol has sometimes been a problem. Britain had to pass special laws to exempt turbaned Sikhs from a law requiring them to wear motorcycle helmets. In America, a still-unresolved court case brought by a Sikh has led the United States Army to consider whether its Sikhs may be permitted to wear the turban with their uniforms.

What Is Sikhism?

The fundamental principle of Sikhism is, "There is only One being and Truth is its Name"— in Punjabi, *Ikk oan kar sat nam.* Sikhs believe in the Divine One, the Supreme Ultimate Reality through which the universe was created and continues to exist. Because of this belief, scholars usually consider Sikhism to be a monotheistic religion. However, unlike followers of Judaism or Christianity, Sikhs never picture a God in whose image they were made, or a Being sitting on a throne in heaven. Nor is the One ever represented by a divine person on earth, such as Christ, Buddha, or Vishnu, the Hindu deity. The Sikh Ultimate Reality is without physical form. It cannot be seen or represented visually in a picture or a statue. It transcends all space, time, and gender. It takes in all other gods and beliefs. Thus the Sikh ideal includes all religions, races, and cultural backgrounds.

Sikhism arises from the teachings of Nanak, the first guru, or teacher, who is believed to have been divinely inspired. Nanak was followed by nine other gurus, all of whom are revered as great teachers and leaders but not worshiped. The words of the gurus are preserved in Sikh scripture, the Guru Granth, the sacred volume that includes the poems and songs of the ten gurus. Sikhs turn to this holy book for inspiration and guidance in ritual and worship, and they treat it with the highest respect.

Sikhs reject ritual and external forms of religion. They focus instead on living their faith. Fellowship, community, and family life are at the center of Sikhism. Sikhs consider other Sikhs to be their brothers and sisters. Sikh travelers to other countries often consult telephone books for Sikh names and then call, knowing

■ *Two Sikh men wear the beard and the turban associated with their religion.*

that they will be welcomed as family. Marriage and children are extremely important to Sikhs. Infidelity is forbidden.

Sikhs do not use tobacco products or any intoxicants, both of which, they believe, harm the mind. But early Sikh gurus rejected the idea that self-denial is necessary to the high ideal of what they called "true living." In India, a country of many vegetarians, most Sikhs eat meat. They enjoy singing, games, and sports events, and their holidays have a festival atmosphere. Wherever Sikhs live, they are involved citizens, working hard and playing hard and trying to live up to the ideals of their faith, which are described as follows:

Worship of the One Ultimate Reality—Sikhs worship what is to them the Ultimate Reality, the timeless, formless force that is above all things and present in all things. They take seriously the words of the scripture to "rejoice in My Name." People may pray anywhere at any time, but many Sikhs feel that at dawn and dusk they can more easily focus their minds on the Ultimate One. Morning and evening prayers are offered in the *gurudwara,* or Sikh house of worship.

Dignity of labor—Earning one's living by honest work and working hard for one's livelihood are good deeds that earn merit toward a better next life. Sikhs do not look down on any kind of work. They find laziness or living off others unacceptable.

Equality of all people—All people are equal because the Divine is present in everyone. Sikhs reject all distinctions of social class, race, and creed because they are artificial and because they separate people from the One Ultimate Reality. Men and women have an equal voice. Everyone is welcome to participate in the life of the Sikh community; no one is excluded.

Service—Sikhs express their beliefs through service to the One by reading from the scriptures and helping with the upkeep of the gurudwara. They also serve the Sikh community by helping fellow Sikhs as brothers and sisters. Finally, they share the fruits of their labor with the poor outside the Sikh community, giving both money and time to charity.

Community—Fellowship is an act of faith. Sikhs everywhere consider themselves to be a family, united through the grace of the Ultimate Reality. They join together regularly for worship and

for community meals and activities. They freely extend hospitality and aid to other Sikhs, both friends and strangers.

The Origins of Sikhism

Sikhs trace their religion to Guru Nanak, a leader whose title, *guru,* means "teacher," or "one who enlightens." The India into which Nanak was born was home to both Hinduism and Islam. Hinduism had originated on the banks of India's Indus River many centuries before, and Islam had come to India from Saudi Arabia in the seventh century C.E. (common era, or after the birth of Christ).

Nanak was born in 1469 C.E. At the time, Europe was experiencing the Renaissance, a time of revival and progress in art,

■ *Following worship, members of a congregation join in preparing* **chapati,** *an Indian bread, to serve at* **langar,** *the Sikh community meal.*

literature, and the sciences. In 1466, the Gutenberg Bible, the first book known to be printed in the Western world, marked the appearance of movable type. This invention spread literacy to an ever wider audience. At the same time, European explorers were voyaging to parts of the world that were unknown on their home continent. In 1492, Christopher Columbus sailed from Spain to search for a westward route to Asia and reached the shores of America. Six years later, the Portuguese explorer Vasco da Gama left Lisbon, sailed around the continent of Africa, and landed on the Arabian seacoast in the Malabar region of south India.

The world of religion, too, was changing. In both East and West, Asia and Europe, people were asking questions: What is the basis of religion? Has this basis been lost over time? Have ritual and ceremony taken the place of faith and devotion? Religious thinkers worried that religion had been reduced to a hollow shell of external form and practice. Fundamentals in religion were being challenged, faults were becoming apparent, and religious leaders were emerging who were reviving old traditions or developing new ones. In Germany, Martin Luther (1483–1546) challenged the teachings of the Christian church and set in motion the wheels of the Reformation, a movement that led to Protestantism. In India, Luther's contemporary, Guru Nanak, provided the impulse for a new and vital religious tradition.

By 1500, when Nanak began teaching, both Hinduism and Islam had enriched Indian thought with their devotional literature, art, and spirituality. Many scholars find traces of both Hinduism and Islam in Sikhism. They point in particular to echoes of the work of Kabir (1440–1518). Both poet and religious reformer, Kabir drew together aspects of the Hindu Bhakti movement and Islamic Sufism. The Hindu Bhaktas stressed the belief that God is the only reality, and they rejected the rigid social structures and rituals of other forms of Hinduism. The Muslim Sufis were mystics who believed in merging the individual self with the One Universal Being. Sikhism shares these elements, and indeed, it has similarities to Christianity, Buddhism, and Taoism as well. However, for the Sikhs, Nanak was clearly the founder of a separate and distinct religious tradition, the first of a line of gurus who underscored his special understanding.

The Guru Granth

The leadership of Guru Nanak passed successively to nine other gurus, each of whom became, in turn, a spiritual leader of the Sikhs. In 1604, the fifth guru, Arjan, compiled a *granth*, a "book" or "sacred volume." In it he collected the poems and songs of the earlier gurus and added his own to the collection. He also included the works of several Muslim and Hindu holy men such as Kabir. A little over one hundred years later, in 1708, the tenth guru, Gobind Singh, decreed that from then on, there would be no other gurus. The granth would be the only guru. Since then, the focus of Sikh ritual and worship has been the Guru Granth. Sikh ceremonies relating to birth, initiation, marriage, and death take place in its presence.

Sikhs and Militancy

Early in their history, the Sikhs were forced by religious persecution and by the execution of two of their gurus by Muslim rulers, to arm themselves for protection. In 1699, Guru Gobind Singh organized an elite fighting force, the *Khalsa*, or "Pure Ones." The members of the Khalsa swore to have faith in the One Reality, to consider all human beings equal, regardless of their religion or social level, and to help the poor and defend the faith. Gobind Singh gave the first five members of the Khalsa the last name *Singh* to signify their equality. He also announced the five symbols that would mark them as members of the Khalsa, thus distinguishing them from non-Sikhs. The most important symbol was *kesha*, or "hair," which was to remain uncut to provide a distinct identity. Thus, Sikhs allow their hair and beards to grow unshorn. The other four symbols were *kangha*, or "comb," for neatness; *kara*, a steel "bracelet" to be worn on the right arm as a symbol of strength and the unbroken circle of Oneness; *kaccha*, or "drawers," a pair of loose shorts worn as an undergarment by soldiers; and *kirpan*, or "sword," a symbol of self-defense and the fight against injustice. These external signs of Sikh faith are known as the *Five Ks* and are now worn by all Sikhs, both men and women.

The Sikh fighting forces have had a long and proud history of military discipline and courage in battle. They remained undefeated until the mid-1800s, when India came under the rule of the British Empire. A period of relative calm followed, during which the Sikhs lived peacefully in the Punjab. Under British rule, many Sikhs acquired land, and the area prospered.

Sikhs fought as part of the British Army in World War I and achieved distinction. After the war, however, disputes about control of Sikh holy places caused unrest. In 1919, the British denied Sikhs permission to gather for a New Year festival. When the Sikhs refused to obey, the British fired on them, killing hundreds. In 1925, matters improved slightly when the government gave Sikhs a voice in the management of their own shrines. A period of uneasy peace followed until World War II, when the Sikhs again fought alongside the British, again with honor.

After World War II, the British left India, and as part of the general peace agreement, a new country, Pakistan, was carved out of the Punjab. Over 2,500,000 Sikhs found themselves in a Muslim country that did not want them. They were forced to leave their homes and move over the border to less desirable land in India. The discontent that resulted eventually led to a movement for a separate Sikh state. By the early 1980s, tensions between the Indian government and the Sikh separatists had worsened to the point of violence. In 1984, a large band of Sikh separatists took refuge in the Golden Temple, one of the Sikh holy places. The Indian Army attacked them there, killing several hundred Sikhs and seriously damaging the temple compound.

The violation of the Golden Temple remains a painful memory for many Sikhs in the Punjab. Yet the majority see the problem with the government as political, not religious. Many Sikhs, whether or not they desire independence from India, feel that they could do a better job of administering their own affairs than has been done by the central government in New Delhi. They contrast the government's oppressive policies with the Sikh way of tolerance and inclusiveness. In resisting oppression and standing up for themselves, Sikhs are being true to the teachings of their gurus, who never opposed any other religions. Rather they rejected political oppression of religion in all its forms.

Despite the image of militancy that has followed them, the Sikhs' message is one of universal love and peace. The concept of *sahaj*, or tranquillity, is central to Guru Nanak's view of the world.

For those who cultivate it, sahaj creates an inner peace and points the way to union with the transcendent reality, the One of Sikhism. At the same time, it creates an outer good will and leads the individual along paths of peaceful interaction with others. The Hindu ideal of shanti, the Jewish ideal of shalom, and the Islamic ideal of salam are all included in the Sikh yearning for sahaj. The search for sahaj is part of the quest for peace and the Ultimate.

Sikhs today continue to believe in the Universal Oneness of all Reality and in the equality of all people. Their message of human fellowship amid diversity of race, culture, and belief is an important one for the modern world.

CHAPTER 2

Guru Nanak and the Origins of the Sikh Faith

anak was the first guru of the Sikh religion. Nanak showed people a new way of understanding the Ultimate Reality, the Divine One of the universe. His vision became the way of the Sikhs.

Nanak was born on November 29, 1469, in Talwandi, a small Indian village in what is now Pakistan. At the time of Nanak's birth, India was ruled by the Muslims. Nanak's family, however, was Hindu. Indian society was organized according to the *caste system*, a rigid system of social order. A *caste* is a social group whose members' rank in society is determined by birth. The castes in India ranged from the Brahmans, who were priests and scholars, down to a group whose rank in society was so low that its people were known as Untouchables.

Nanak was born into one of the higher castes and was named after his older sister, Nanaki. His father was an accountant for the local Muslim landlord. Nanak's mother was known as a pious and gentle woman.

By Nanak's lifetime, the tradition of keeping of written records was well established in Europe and Asia. Thus, there are

many contemporary accounts of Nanak's life and teachings from people who actually saw and heard him. In the sixteenth century, not long after Nanak's death, his followers wrote short narratives about his birth and life. These narratives, or stories, are the first works of prose in Punjabi, the language of the Punjab, and they are called *Janamsakhi*, from the Punjabi words *janam*, which means "birth," and *sakhi*, which means "story." The writers came from different traditions and social groups, but they all believed that Nanak's life was unique.

Nanak's Birth and Early Life

According to the *Janamsakhi* stories, Nanak's life had much in common with the lives of Moses, Jesus, Buddha, and Krishna. The births of great religious leaders have often been marked by wonderful predictions and events. The prophets told Buddha's father, King Sudhodhan, that his child would be a great king or a great saint. The three Wise Men followed a bright star to honor the baby Jesus, born in a stable in Bethlehem. And just as that stable was lighted by the bright Star of Bethlehem, the humble mud hut in which Nanak was born was flooded with light at the moment of his birth.

The family priest had predicted that the newborn child, Nanak, would be a great seer, or prophet:

> *Both Hindus and Muslims will venerate him.*
> *His name will become known on earth and in heaven.*
> *The ocean will give him way: so will the earth and*
> *the sky. He will worship only one Formless God*
> *and teach others to do so. He will hold all men*
> *equal as God's creation.*

His early life was marked by the conflicts between Muslims and Hindus. Yet even as a child, Nanak was spreading peace and good will. The *Janamsakhi* stories record that both Hindus and Muslims were impressed with the boy:

> *If a Hindu saw him, he would exclaim: "Great is*
> *our Lord, Vishnu! Here is such a small child and*
> *yet he speaks so nobly. His words are as holy as*

*he is handsome. He is the image of God Himself."
And if a Muslim saw him, he would say: "Wonderful
is your creation, Merciful Master! How good looking
is the child and how polite is his speech. Talking to
him brings one such satisfaction. He is a noble one
blessed by the Almighty Allah."*

When he was seven years old, Nanak's father took him first
to the Hindu priest of the village to begin his education and then
to a school run by a Hindu teacher. For a while, Nanak also
attended a school kept by a Muslim priest. The boy proved to be
an uncommonly bright and promising student. His teachers were
surprised at his ability to grasp difficult ideas. Soon teachers from
both Hindu and Muslim traditions came to realize that there was
nothing further they could teach him.

One of the features of the Hindu religion is a belief in rein-
carnation, or earthly rebirth, to increasingly higher levels of existence. Someone from a low caste may hope that his or her actions
in the present will allow rebirth to a higher caste in his or her next
life. Someone from a high caste is believed to be twice-born—that
is, to have gone through a cycle of birth and death. Hindu males
from the upper castes wear a "sacred thread," a cord that symbolizes rebirth and distinguishes them from the Untouchables.

According to the *Janamsakhi* stories, Nanak, like all Hindu
boys, was required at the age of eleven to participate in an initiation ritual in which he would put on the sacred thread. When the
priest called on him, he refused. His answer to the priest has
become a famous Sikh hymn:

*Let compassion be your cotton;
Spin it into yarn of contentment
Give it knots of continence
And the twists of truth.
Thus will you make a sacred thread for the soul;
If such a one you have,
Put it on me.*

Thus, even at a very early age, Nanak expressed opposition
to ritual and to the caste system that limited the freedom of people

in his society. In a time when many Hindus and Muslims were focusing on external ceremony and ritual, Nanak was inclined toward the life of the spirit.

Nanak lost interest in formal education. He left school and turned his attention to contemplating the Divine. But where others perceived the spark of divinity, Nanak's father saw only a teen-ager who would not attend school. Wanting the boy to make himself useful, he sent Nanak to the fields to graze cattle. Soon the village of Talwandi was abuzz with accounts of Nanak the herder having the power to work miracles.

A *Janamsakhi* story tells us that one day, while he was grazing the cattle, Nanak sat on the ground, rapt in the beauty of nature. The cattle he was supposed to be watching strayed into a neighbor's wheat field and quickly devoured the crop. The farmer was enraged. He angrily complained to the village chief, and soon a delegation came to assess the damage. To their amazement, not a blade of wheat was gone, and "the field seemed to proclaim that if any damage had been done, it must be elsewhere." The farmer had seen with his own eyes the chomping cattle in the midst of the ruined crop. Now he saw his crop perfectly restored. He humbly admitted that a miracle of God had taken place.

On another occasion, Nanak lay down one summer day to rest under a tree. He fell asleep. The sun slowly rose to its highest point, and the shade of the tree retreated, leaving the sleeping Nanak exposed to the direct rays of the scorching midday sun. While Nanak slept, a cobra, one of India's deadliest snakes, slid from a nearby hole. It spread its hood to shade Nanak's face from the burning sun. A town official observed the event, and marveling at what he had seen, carried the news back to the townspeople.

These stories and others from the *Janamsakhi* portray the extraordinary dimension of Nanak's life. The simple narratives illustrate his religious and ethical teachings. They also incorporate verses from his poems and songs. Sikhs both young and old read and retell the *Janamsakhi* stories. In many Sikh households, parents and grandparents read these stories at bedtime to young children.

Nanak's Divine Calling

When he was a young man, Nanak moved to the city of Sultanpur to live with his sister Nanaki and her husband. In the city, he worked in a store owned by the local Muslim landlord, and to the landlord's dismay, he often gave away goods without charging for them. Yet Nanak's generosity did not deplete the store's supplies. When Nanak was called to account for his actions, it was found that nothing was missing.

One morning, as was his custom, Nanak went to bathe in the River Bein. When he did not return, his family and friends began to search for him. His clothes were found on the riverbank, but there was no sign of the young man anywhere. Everyone believed that he had drowned in the river. Nanak was beloved by all, and the entire city was plunged into gloom.

On the third day, Nanak returned. He explained that during his absence, he had been in direct communion with the Ultimate Reality, the Divine One. The *Janamsakhi* recounts Nanak's vision:

> As the Almighty willed, Nanak the devotee was
> ushered into the Divine Presence. Then a cup filled
> with amrit [nectar] was given him with the command,
> "Nanak, this is the cup of Name-Adoration. Drink it. . . .
> I am with you and I do bless and exalt you. Whoever
> remembers you will have my favor. Go, rejoice, in My
> Name, and teach others to do so. . . . I have bestowed
> upon you the gift of My Name. Let this be your calling."
> Nanak offered his salutations and stood up.

Nanak experienced the Ultimate Reality as without form and transcendent, above all things. He did not actually see the Ultimate Reality in any concrete form. He heard the divine words, the cup of nectar appeared before him, and he drank from it. Thus began the Sikh religion. This account portrays Nanak's revelation as unique but one that his followers can also experience for themselves.

Nanak's Message

When Nanak first emerged from the river, he pronounced the words that would form the foundation of Sikhism: "There is

■ *A bas relief on a temple wall depicts Guru Nanak and the two beloved disciples who accompanied him on his travels: Mardana, a Muslim musician, and his childhood friend Bala, a Hindu poet.*

no Hindu; there is no Muslim." Thus, in one sentence, Nanak rejected all religious and sectarian distinctions among human beings. The statement does not deny the variety and richness of religious beliefs. Rather it embraces them all and celebrates the shared basis of all humanity. The vision of the Infinite One enabled Nanak to recognize the unity of society beyond narrow categories such as Hindu and Muslim, or for that matter, Jew, Christian, or Buddhist. His encounter with the Divine had showed him that all religions taught one true message—that of devotion to the One Reality.

Nanak set out to teach this message of the One Reality and the one fellowship of humanity. He was then twenty-eight years old, married to a woman named Sulakhni, and the father of two sons, Sri Chand and Lakhmi Chand. But the call to spread the Divine Word was strong in him, and for the next twenty-five years, his travels took him not only throughout India but also to such faraway places as Iraq and Saudi Arabia and even to Mecca, the holy city of Islam. Nanak was accompanied on his journeys by Mardana, a Muslim family servant and musician, who played the *rebec*, a three-stringed musical instrument, while Nanak composed and sang songs full of love for the Divine One. Mardana put Nanak's songs to music and the two organized community singing.

Bhai Gurdas, a contemporary of Guru Arjan, and a highly esteemed Sikh historian and poet, records that Nanak visited the Hindus, Muslims, and Buddhists and discussed with them their respective scriptures and philosophies. Wherever Nanak went, he taught an inner way of reaching the Divine. He exhorted people to discard external rituals and ceremonies. He did not ask others to renounce their religious faith, because to him it did not matter whether they were Hindu or Muslim. The important thing was that they believed in the One Reality and were kind to all.

Nanak's teaching drew people from different religions, cultures, and levels of society. Wherever he went, people began to follow him, won over by his simple, direct manner and his liberal, universal message. These followers came to be known as *Sishyas*, the word in the Sanskrit language for "disciples," and eventually came to be called *Sikhs*.

At the end of his travels, Nanak settled on the right bank of the River Ravi in the Punjab. There he founded a village called Kartarpur. A community of disciples grew around him there, but its members did not take vows or live as monks and nuns. The community was not monastic; it was a fellowship of men and women engaged in the ordinary occupations of life but devoted to the teachings of Nanak. So from its earliest beginnings, Sikhism was not just a religion, it was also a way of life, extending to all phases of human conduct.

The Elements of Sikhism

At Kartarpur, Nanak established three important elements of Sikh religious and social discipline: *seva, langar,* and *sangat.* These elements have been strong factors in encouraging the Sikh values of equality, fellowship, and humility, and in affirming a sense of "familyhood."

Seva is voluntary manual labor in the service of the community. It is the performance of a deed of love and selfless service that contributes the work of one's hands to serving fellow human beings, both within and outside the Sikh community. Seva is the highest ideal in Sikh ethics. Through seva, Sikh believers cultivate humility, overcome ego, and purify their body and mind. Seva is an essential condition of spiritual discipline. Nanak taught that "by practicing deeds of humble and devoted service alone does one earn a seat in the next world." Serving others with a cheerful attitude is deeply cherished.

Over the centuries, seva has become an essential part of Sikh life. It may take the form of attending to the holy book, sweeping and dusting the shrines, preparing and serving food, or looking after and even cleaning the shoes of worshipers. Young and old, rich and poor, each takes on and performs different tasks. Seva also includes serving the community at large by helping to build schools, hospitals, and charity homes. It goes beyond serving fellow Sikhs. It is extended to all, friend and enemy alike. One Sikh account tells the story of a Sikh soldier named Ghanaya in the army of Guru Gobind Singh. His fellow soldiers saw him giving water to fallen enemies and reported him to the guru. Ghanaya was called in and questioned. He responded that as he moved about the battlefield, he had seen neither friend nor foe but only the guru's face. According to this account, the guru gave him medicines and bandages and sent him back to help the wounded. Sikhs point to these actions as an example of nonpartisan, humanitarian aid to the victims of war that predates the Red Cross and the Red Crescent by centuries.

Langar is both the community meal and the kitchen in which it is prepared. Langar is a central part of Sikhism. It testifies to the social equality and familyhood of all people. This fundamental Sikh institution involves the process of preparing meals together as well as eating together. The food used at langar is vegetarian so as not to cause offense to anyone. Both men and women engage in preparation and cleanup—chopping vegetables, kneading and rolling out dough, cleaning utensils. Then they sit in a *pangat,* or long row, without regard to caste, race, or religion, and they eat the meal that they have prepared together.

In Nanak's time, the idea of different castes eating together was bold and revolutionary. Yet Nanak understood the importance of a shared meal in creating a feeling of belonging and fellowship. Like the Thanksgiving feast or the Christmas dinner, like the Jewish Seder or the other traditional meals, all of which are shared with those people who are close to us or part of a community, langar creates a feeling of family. It extends the concept of the family meal as a step toward bonding human beings, regardless of race, gender, caste, and class.

The langar as an instrument of social change continued to gain importance under the leadership of the successive gurus. In Guru Angad's day, his wife, Mata Khivi, was known for the rich and delicious meals she served. The third guru, Amar Das, insisted that visitors first enjoy langar with the community before

■ *A Sikh congregation in Delhi, India, participates in* **langar,** *the community meal, after a worship service. To show equality, people sit together in long rows rather than at tables, and all begin eating at once.*

meeting with him. "First pangat, then meeting with the guru," he decreed.

Sikhs consider langar to be a way of earning merit toward rebirth and their next life. In modern times, the custom is still very much in evidence in India, not only in the gurudwaras but beyond. During certain celebrations, such as the birthday of a guru, the celebration of an important historical event, or the martyrdom of a Sikh hero, langar is everywhere, even on the highways and byways. Sikhs of all ages arrange themselves in rows to block the road or they lay tree trunks across it to stop the flow of traffic. They stop the speeding buses, cars, and trucks, the slow-going bullock-carts, rickshaws, and pedestrians, and they enthusiastically serve langar to the drivers and passengers.

Sangat is the Sikh gathering, or local community. Sikhs prize comradeship and company with others, and the fellowship of the sangat is of primary importance in their religious practice. The tradition of an active and fruitful involvement with the community comes from Nanak himself, and Sikhs see community participation as an essential part of their faith. According to a popular Sikh saying, "One disciple is a single Sikh, two form a holy association, but where there are five present, there is the Ultimate Reality Itself."

Like langar, sangat is open to all. Members of Sikh congregations sit on the floor, singing hymns, listening to readings from the holy text, reciting verses, and praying, with no restrictions as to race, creed, or caste. The inclusive nature of sangat dates to the time of Nanak, who welcomed everyone who wished to follow him. The historian Bhai Gurdas notes that wherever Nanak went, sangat soon emerged. Bhai Gurdas describes the daily schedule at Kartarpur, with the community gathering for evening hymns and morning prayers: "In the evening arti and sohila were sung and in the morning was recited the Jap."

Sangat is a mode of both spiritual and moral inspiration. According to Nanak: "Through sangat, one obtains the treasure of the Divine Name. . . . Just as iron rubbed against the philosopher's stone turns into gold, so does dark ignorance transform into brilliant light in company of the good." Participation with others becomes a force for inspiring the spiritual quest.

The three institutions fostered by Guru Nanak—seva, langar, and sangat—have remained important social and religious structures for the Sikhs. Through them, Guru Nanak's followers formed a tightly knit community that has evolved into a distinct Sikh identity.

The Tradition of the Gurus

At the end of his life, Nanak established yet another tradition of far-reaching importance for the Sikhs. He called one of his faithful disciples, Lehna, to him and gave him the name Angad, which literally means "a part of his own self." Nanak placed five copper coins and a coconut before Lehna and bowed down at his feet. Thus, Lehna became Guru Angad, the second guru in Sikh history and the new leader of the Sikh community.

Sikhs believe that by naming him Angad, Nanak had made Lehna more than his successor. He had transferred his own inner light to Lehna, making Lehna one with him in spirit. The Sikh scripture describes the transference as being like one flame kindling another. The light and the message had passed from Nanak to Angad. This transference, begun by Nanak, was repeated successively through the installation of the tenth guru, Gobind Singh, in 1675.

The ten gurus of the Sikh tradition are unique in the history of religion. The same light is reflected in ten different bodies, and the same voice speaks through all ten. However, the guru in Sikhism does not represent the Ultimate Reality in any way. The guru is not divine, nor is he a Christlike figure. The guru is a channel, a guide who enlightens people and enables them to understand the love and nature of the Divine Reality.

The tenth guru, Gobind Singh, ended the line of personal gurus by passing the succession not to another person but to the Guru Granth, the holy book of the Sikhs. From that time on, the light and voice of the Ultimate Reality have been transmitted by the scriptures. Thus the message and the mission begun by Guru Nanak continued through nine more gurus and reached culmination in the Guru Granth.

Nanak died on September 7, 1539. The *Janamsakhi* story records that after Nanak's death, his sheet-covered body was

■ **The Ten Gurus of Sikhism**
Guru Nanak
  (1469–1539)
Guru Angad
  (1539–1552)
Guru Amar Das
  (1552–1574)
Guru Ram Das
  (1574–1581)
Guru Arjan
  (1581–1606)
Guru Hargobind
  (1606–1644)
Guru Har Rai
  (1644–1661)
Guru Har Krishan
  (1661–1664)
Guru Tegh Bahadur
  (1664–1675)
Guru Gobind Singh
  (1675–1708)

■ *Guru Nanak, founder of the Sikh religion.*

claimed by both Hindus and Muslims, each group wanting to perform the last rites. According to their customs, the Hindus wanted to cremate Nanak's body, the Muslims, to bury it. But when the sheet was pulled away, nothing was there but flowers.

According to the story, the sheet and the flowers were divided between the Muslims and the Hindus, to be disposed of according to the beliefs of each group. The body of Nanak had vanished, leaving behind the message of universal harmony for generations to come.

CHAPTER 3

Sikh Tradition and the Guru Granth

*T*he Guru Granth, the holy book of the Sikhs, is 1,430 pages long and is written entirely in verse. It is the longest book of rhymed poetry in the world. The word *granth* simply means "book," and *guru* signifies that this particular granth has been designated the "guru," or giver of enlightenment for all Sikhs. The Guru Granth is the focal point of all Sikh rituals and ceremonies. Wherever it rests, that space becomes holy.

The Compiling of the Guru Granth

After Nanak's divine revelation at the River Bein, he sang a song of joy. Throughout his ministry, inspired by the Divine One, he sang and recited many more verses. The sacred songs of Nanak were the beginning of Sikh scripture.

Nanak's poems express a range of experience, from great joy to deep grief. They tell of his longing to be united with the Inifinite Divine One, his awe at the grandeur and vastness of creation, and his sympathy for fellow beings in bondage and oppression. Sikhs believe that Nanak's poetry was not consciously created but sprang spontaneously from his lips. As he spoke, his followers copied

down the holy words. All believed his words to be divinely inspired: "[T]o you belong my breath, to you my flesh," says the poet Nanak, "you the True One are my Beloved."

The Sikh historian Bhai Gurdas says that Nanak carried a manuscript of his poems with him. The *Janamsakhi* records that before his death, Nanak passed his Word, recorded in book form, to his successor, Angad.

When Angad inherited the guruship from Nanak, he continued the tradition of sacred poetry, which he felt was important for the beauty it brought to human life as well as for the knowledge it transmitted. "It is ambrosia [heavenly nectar], it is the essence of all, it emerges from deep knowledge and intense concentration," Angad wrote. To record the sacred word, Angad developed a written form of the Punjabi language, *Gurmukhi* script. He added his own poetry to that of Nanak and signed it with his pseudonym—Nanak.

As the guruship passed successively from one guru to the next, so did each guru's words. Each guru valued and preserved the literary inheritance from those before him and thus each passed the body of poetry to the next after adding his own poetry. Each guru signed his composition with the name Nanak. In that way, each affirmed his unity with Nanak, who continued to speak through all of them. The third guru, Amar Das, another of Guru Nanak's disciples, not only added his own poetic compositions and songs but also included those of some of the Hindu saints. The two volumes he collected survive to this day.

By 1603, Sikhism was no longer contained in one small area. It had spread geographically and grown in its numbers. During a famine in the Punjab, Guru Arjan had traveled widely, from village to village, helping to sink wells and performing other kinds of public service. As a result, many people had joined the Sikh *panth,* or community. They needed a common message for their spiritual and moral life, a text that would give a single, definite form to Sikh beliefs.

And then there was the problem of counterfeit works. The Guru Granth was supposed to record the words of Nanak and the gurus who had directly succeeded him, but the succession was not completely free of problems. Ram Das, the fourth guru, had by-passed his older sons and appointed his younger son, Arjan, to the guruship. But Pirthi Chand, Arjan's eldest brother, and Pirthi's son Meharban were composing sacred poetry and signing it with the name Nanak. Arjan feared that the words of his predecessors would become diluted.

Arjan, the fifth guru, undertook the job of compiling an authorized version of the holy Guru Granth. He began to draw the Sikh literary legacy into an authorized volume for coming generations. The task was a difficult one. Arjan called on the historian Bhai Gurdas for help. They chose a serene and picturesque spot in a forest outside the town of Amritsar in which to work. Today, this site near the Pakistani border is marked by a shrine called Ramsar.

By now, a vast amount of poetry had been handed down. Arjan himself had composed thousands of hymns. Selections had to be made from his poems as well as from the works of the

---

■ Contributors to the Guru Granth
The Sikh Gurus
Guru Nanak: 974 hymns
Guru Angad: 62 couplets
Guru Amar Das: 907 hymns
Guru Ram Das: 638 hymns
Guru Arjan: 2,218 hymns
Guru Tegh Bahadur: 59 hymns and 56 couplets
  (added by Guru Gobind Singh)

Bhaktas and Sufis

Kabir: 292 hymns and 243 couplets	*Dhanna: 4 hymns*
Farid: 4 hymns and 130 couplets	*Pipa: 1 hymn*
Namdev: 60 hymns	*Sain: 1 hymn*
Ravidas: 41 hymns	*Bhikhan: 2 hymns*
Jaidev: 2 hymns	*Sur Das: 2 hymns*
Beni: 3 hymns	*Sundar: 1 hymn*
Trilochan: 4 hymns	*Mardana: 3 couplets*
Parmananda: 1 hymn	*Satta and Balvand: 1 hymn*
Sadhana: 1 hymn	*Bhatts: 123 swatyyas (quatrains)*
Ramananda: 1 hymn	

preceding four gurus. In addition, Arjan wanted to represent Hindu and Muslim saints whose works were in harmony with Sikh belief. Finally, what was genuine had to be sifted from what was not. As they worked, Bhai Gurdas copied the chosen pieces in *Gurmukhi* script.

Arjan arranged the selected compositions according to their musical patterns. Except for a few poems that he left to stand alone, Arjan organized the collection into thirty-one sections. Each section contains poems written in one *raga*, or melody pattern—a form in Hindu music having the melodic rhythm prescribed by tradition. The ragas appear in a particular order. Each raga has its own distinctive intervals, rhythms, and timing, and each is associated with a particular season of the year. For instance, the first raga is *Sri*, which means "supreme." It is a basic melody pattern from which others are derived. The Sikhs compare Sri to the philosopher's stone, an imaginary substance that ancient people believed could transform base metals such as iron into gold. Sri is sung in the evening, the time of advancing darkness. In content, too, it expresses the darkness of ignorance and superstition in society before Nanak's ministry. Sri is also associated with extreme heat and cold or extremes of emotion. The hymns in the Sri pattern express a great yearning for the Divine.

Within each of the thirty-one sections of the Guru Granth, Arjan arranged the compositions in a particular order. First came the works of the earlier gurus in the order of their succession. Since all of the gurus had signed their poems Nanak, Arjan distinguished them by using the word *Mahalla*, which means "body," and a number. Thus, poems headed *Mahalla 1* were the work of the first guru, those headed *Mahalla 2* were the work of the second guru, and so on. This designation symbolized the belief that each guru shared the spirit of Nanak in his body. After the gurus' poems, Arjan placed the works of a number of Hindu saints and one Muslim, Sheikh Farid.

The completion of the Guru Granth was an occasion of great celebration. On August 16, 1604, Sikhs traveled for miles to witness the colorful procession that would bear the sacred volume to Harimandir, the temple at Amritsar. Harimandir, a special place for Sikh worship, was the inspiration of Amar Das, the third guru.

■ *A Sikh guard stands on the causeway of marble tiles leading across the reflecting pool to the Golden Temple at Amritsar.*

Work on Harimandir had begun under Ram Das, the fourth guru, in 1577. A structure of great architectural beauty that drew on both Hindu and Muslim design, the temple had been completed in 1601, only three years before the completion of the Guru Granth. Harimandir came to be known as the Golden Temple after the Sikh maharaja Ranjit Singh had it reconstructed and plated with gold.

An elderly and much respected Sikh follower, Bhai Buddha, carried the Guru Granth on his head. Arjan walked behind, holding a whisk over the holy book to shade and protect it. Musicians played hymns from its pages. Observers likened the atmosphere to that of a joyous wedding.

Once inside, Bhai Buddha reverently opened the Guru Granth to obtain the *hukm,* or Divine Command, while Arjan stood in attendance. At dusk, the Guru Granth was taken to a special chamber and placed on a pedestal. Arjan remained with it, sleeping on the floor by its side to show the esteem in which he held it. This original Guru Granth is preserved today at Kartarpur, a town near Jalandhar, founded by Guru Arjan.

Thus, during Arjan's time, the Sikhs acquired both a sacred space in which to worship and a sacred text to guide them. Both helped to mold the Sikhs' consciousness of themselves and their faith. The Golden Temple at Amritsar provided a central place for gathering and worship. The Guru Granth gave the Sikh message concrete form. Their holy book not only became their spiritual and religious guide, but it also shaped their intellectual and cultural environment.

The Rise of Sikh Militarism

As the Sikh faith took form and its followers grew in number, the Muslim rulers of India began to see them as a threat. Arjan was imprisoned by the Mogul governor of the Punjab, and, in 1606, he was tortured to death. The Sikhs viewed Arjan as a martyr to the faith, and his death generated a strong impulse for self-defense.

Arjan's son, Hargobind, succeeded him as guru. On the day that he was to be invested, Hargobind appeared dressed as a warrior. He put on two swords. The sword of *piri* symbolized the spiritual power of guruship; the sword of *miri* symbolized earthly power. Together, the swords represented the joining of the heavenly and earthly aspects of Sikhism. With that action, a new era began. The meekness and gentleness that had characterized the Sikh population was replaced by armed resistance.

Hargobind raised a small, armed band of Sikhs and let it be known that future disciples were to come bearing gifts of horses and weapons. In 1609, he built a fortress called the Iron Fort to defend the town of Amritsar. In front of the Golden Temple, he built the *Akal Takht,* or "Throne of the Timeless One." Harimandir, the Golden Temple, was for prayer alone. Secular, or nonreligious, affairs would be conducted from the Akal Takht.

This martial atmosphere intensified after the death of Tegh Bahadur, the ninth guru. Tegh Bahadur had come to the defense of the Hindu population, whom the Muslim rulers were forcing to convert to Islam. For his stand on religious freedom, Tegh Bahadur was imprisoned and beheaded in 1675. His son, Gobind Singh, was only nine years old at the time. Nevertheless, he became the tenth guru and carried on the moral and spiritual legacy with great fervor.

The Founding of the Khalsa

On March 30, 1699, on *Baisakhi,* the Indian New Year's Day, Guru Gobind Singh called his people together at Anandpur, a town in the Shivalik hills. According to the accounts of contemporary Sikh historians, large numbers of Sikhs arrived for the festival and an air of anticipation ran through the crowd. At last Gobind Singh appeared, dressed in full battle gear and carrying a gleaming sword. The guru reminded the people of the need for unity and courage against persecution. Then, holding up his weapon, he cried, "My sword today wants a head. Let any one of my true Sikhs come forward."

Gobind Singh's singular demand numbed the assembly. For a long moment, no one moved, no one uttered a word. Gobind Singh repeated his words. People were stunned. They could not believe their ears. The guru wanted one of them to volunteer to die! Confusion turned to fear, and a murmur of dismay ran through the gathered crowd.

The guru repeated the call. This time, a man stood up. His name was Daya Ram, and he was a Hindu. He walked forward, and Gobind Singh escorted him into a nearby tent.

The crowd waited—but not for long. Gobind Singh emerged from the tent, his sword dripping with blood. To the horror of the onlookers, he called for another head. This was more than the people could endure. Many began to leave. Some asked the guru's mother to stop him. But another man, Dharam Das, stood up to offer himself to the guru's sword.

He, too, was escorted into the tent, and again the guru returned with a bloodied sword. Now he demanded a third head. Five times in all, Gobind Singh led a man into the tent, and four times he returned to the horrified crowd with his sword dripping blood. They had seen Mokham Chand, Himmat, and Sahib Chand follow the first two men into the tent. When would it end? Then the guru reappeared with all five men, now dressed like the guru himself in military garb and wearing swords of their own. The guru thus introduced the courageous *Panj Pyare*, or "Five Beloved," who had been willing to follow their guru, even to death.

These five men became the first members of the Khalsa—the "Pure Ones." By their willingness to die for their faith, they were reborn into a new order, a brotherhood with the guru himself. Membership in this new order severed all previous family ties, and each member received a new surname: Singh, meaning "lion." No longer would these men be bound by the restrictions of their castes, hereditary occupations, or earlier rituals. They swore to fight fearlessly and to give their lives willingly for their faith, to have faith in the One, and to consider all human beings equal, without regard to caste or religion. Gobind Singh spoke the following words:

> *I wish you all to embrace one creed and follow one path,*
> *rising above all differences of religion as now practiced.*
> *Let the four Hindu castes, who have different duties*
> *laid down for them in their scriptures, abandon them*
> *altogether, and adopting the way of mutual help and*
> *cooperation, mix freely with one another. Do not follow*
> *the old scriptures. Let none pay homage to the Ganges*

■ *Modern-day Sikh militants in India show their commitment by dressing in the tunic and shawl that were worn by the Khalsa in Guru Go-bind Singh's day.*

> *and other places of pilgrimage which are considered to be holy in the Hindu religion, or worship the Hindu deities such as Rama, Krishna, Brahma, and Durga, and so forth, but all should cherish faith in the teachings of Guru Nanak and his successors. Let each of the four castes receive my Baptism of the double-edged sword, eat out of the same vessel, and feel no aloofness from, or contempt for, one another.*

The guru poured water into a steel bowl and stirred it with his sword, chanting verses from the Guru Granth. His wife dropped some sugar into the bowl, and its sweetness mingled with the touch of steel, creating *amrit*, the nectar used in the Sikh baptism ritual. The five then drank from the same bowl, sealing their pledge of equality and faithfulness.

The guru then told the five men of the Five Ks, the external Khalsa symbols that would mark them as Sikhs: *kesha,* uncut hair and beard, would show their obedience to the way of nature; *kangha,* a comb, would set them apart from the Indian recluses whose tangled, matted hair was seen as an indication that they had renounced the world and were living in seclusion, apart from society; *kara,* a steel bracelet, would symbolize strength and continuity; *kaccha,* loose shorts worn by soldiers of the time, would symbolize chastity and moral restraint; and *kirpan,* a sword, would symbolize the fight against oppression.

In creating the Khalsa, Gobind Singh gave practical form to Nanak's vision of the Oneness of Ultimate Reality and the Oneness of all people. He called on the faithful to "recognize the singular caste of humanity," words that are still recited by Sikhs everywhere. He made the Amrit ceremony, or baptism, available to both men and women, and invited the women to wear the symbols of the Khalsa, too. As men would receive the surname Singh, women would receive the surname Kaur, meaning "princess," which they would retain even after they married. Gobind Singh's declaration thus changed the patriarchal structure of Sikh society. From that time on, men and women no longer traced their ancestry to their fathers. As Singh and Kaur, both became equal partners in the new family of Sikhism.

The Granth Is Named Guru

Contemporary Sikh historians record the passing of the holy authority of guru from Gobind Singh to the Guru Granth. According to their accounts, on October 6, 1708, Guru Gobind Singh lay dying. He had not yet named a successor, and his disciples wondered on whom the mantle of guruship would fall. At last the guru called for the Guru Granth. When his disciples brought the holy book to him, Gobind Singh placed a coin and a coconut before it, much as Nanak had done in naming Angad Guru. Gobind Singh bowed his head in reverence. Then he commanded the gathered community to acknowledge the Guru Granth as the guru in his place. The Guru Granth thus became the Guru Eternal of the Sikh people, and the line of gurus that had begun with Nanak came to an end. From that day on, Sikhs have revered the Guru Granth as both the Divine Word and the physical representation of their guru. In their daily prayers, morning and evening, Sikhs recite: "Acknowledge the Guru Granth as the visible body of the Gurus."

The Contents of the Guru Granth

The Guru Granth opens with the numeral *One*. It is the first word of the first statement of Guru Nanak: *Ikk Oan Kar*—literally, "One Reality Is," or "There is one Being." All 1,430 pages of the Guru Granth expand on these three words.

Ikk Oan Kar is both a verbal and a visual statement. Like the Christian cross, it serves as a central symbol, depicted on gateways, walls, medallions, canopies, fabric, and even jewelry. *Ikk*, the concept of Oneness, was central to Nanak's vision and to his message. His society was torn by religious conflict that ran counter to the oneness of the Ultimate Reality that Nanak preached. He understood the Ultimate Reality as being without form or image and not confined to space, time, or gender. What human term would describe it? In which language? Instead of writing the word *Ikk* or coining a new word to express oneness, Nanak used the numeral *One* to express the Ultimate Reality. The numeral *One* transcended barriers of language, could be understood by people of all cultures, was visible to all, simple and universal. The second word, *Oan*, or "Reality," is the same as the Sanskrit *Om*. The symbol for the third word, *Kar*, or "Is," is an unending arch that symbolizes the eternal nature of the One that is without beginning or end.

These first three words are the fundamental affirmation of Sikhism. The Guru Granth then describes the Reality, its relation to the world, and its relation to the people of the world. Overall, the Guru Granth contains no historical narratives and no biographical details as do the Jewish and Christian Bibles. It provides no dogma. It prescribes no code of behavior and lists no obligations. The Sikh holy book is composed entirely of spiritually exalted poetry. Its theme is the individual's longing for the Ultimate Reality.

Preparing to read from the Guru Granth, a Sikh follower waves a **chouri**, or whisk, in homage over the holy book.

The Guru Granth ends with the *Mundavani,* the seal, or final word, of its compiler, Guru Arjan:

> *On the platter lie arranged three delicacies:*
> *Truth, contentment, and contemplation . . .*
> *All who eat them, all who savor them*
> *Obtain liberation.*

The Guru Granth invites the Sikhs to partake of its offerings, its "three delicacies" of truth, contentment, and contemplation. Through them, followers may understand the fundamental essence of the universe, satisfy spiritual hunger, and anchor the restless mind and spirit in contemplation. Intellectual understanding is not enough, however. The offerings are also to be savored and enjoyed. The poetry of the Guru Granth calls for an aesthetic experience, a total emotional response from the reader.

In Sikh sacred literature, religion and art merge. Repetition of vowel and consonant sounds, balance, and musical rhythms in the poetry encourage readers to go beyond themselves and to experience personally the Ultimate One that Nanak experienced in the River Bein.

The Guru Granth in Sikh Life

The Guru Granth is the continuing spiritual and historical authority for the Sikhs, as well as the source of their literary inspiration. The community's ideals, institutions, and rituals derive their meaning from it. Ceremonies related to birth, initiation, marriage, and death take place in its presence. Harbans Singh, an eminent Sikh scholar, asserts that the physical presence of the Guru Granth and its poetic contents are the two main forces that have shaped the Sikh's conduct and their sense of what it means to be Sikh.

As the only visible representation of the Sikh religion, the Guru Granth is treated with the highest respect and veneration. In its presence, Sikhs bow before it and remove their shoes and cover their heads. They do it homage by standing before it or by sitting on the floor, lower than the platform on which it rests.

Every day, in Sikh homes and in gurudwaras, Sikhs open the Guru Granth at dawn. This act of opening the holy book is called *prakash*, "making the light manifest." Any baptized Sikh may perform prakash; in Sikh homes, the duty often rotates among family members, and in gurudwaras, among sangat members. The book is draped in rich silk and brocade cloth, called *rumala*, placed on quilted mats, and supported by three cushions, one under each side and one in the center. A canopy hangs over it for protection, and a whisk waves over it as a sign of respect. Those present stand humbly in front of it and recite *ardas*, a prayer of supplication. The Guru Granth is then opened at random, and the passage at the top of the left-hand page is read aloud. This passage is called *vak*, the order or message for the day.

After dusk, the Guru Granth is closed. The closing ritual is called *sukhasan*, which means "to sit comfortably." Again, ardas is

■ *A worshiper pays respects to the Guru Granth as it rests on its **palki,** or throne, a platform decorated with rich fabrics and flowers.*

said and vak taken. Evening prayers are recited, and the Guru Granth is closed.

In times of uncertainty and difficulty or in times of celebration and hope, the Guru Granth is read through from beginning to end. The reading may be *saptah*, a seven-day reading, or it may be *akhand*, a forty-eight-hour, nonstop reading of the Guru Granth, during which several readers, called *Granthis*, take turns reading.

There are other special readings, as well. In *sampat*, one particular hymn is repeated after each passage. A *khulla* reading is one that Sikhs undertake privately, and it may take a month or a year to complete.

Anyone, male or female, who can read *Gurmukhi* script may read the Guru Granth anywhere, perhaps in a gurudwara or perhaps in a private home. Usually, when a family owns a copy of the Guru Granth, the book occupies a special room.

The Sikhs respect the poetry of the Hindu and Muslim saints in the Guru Granth as much as they do the poetry of their gurus. Thus, in their daily practice, the Sikhs continue to live according to Guru Nanak's words: "There is no Hindu; there is no Muslim."

CHAPTER 4

Sikh Thought

The Guru Granth begins with a short passage called the *Mul Mantra*. The few lines in this passage state the essential creed, the basic belief, of the Sikh religion. The Mul Mantra precedes the Jap—the first hymn composed by Guru Nanak—and devout Sikhs recite the thirty-eight stanzas of the Jap every morning. In a shortened version, the Mul Mantra can also be found introducing many different sections of the Guru Granth. The Mul Mantra is the nucleus of Sikh thought.

Like other mantras, the Mul Mantra is a portion of a prayer of special beauty and power. It is rhythmic and brief. Great meaning is packed into its few words. In the original Punjabi, it is not written in sentences but in a few individual words and images that together express the fundamental focus of Sikhism. In these few words and images, the Mul Mantra expresses Sikh metaphysics—the belief in the nature of being and reality and the relationship of individuals to the universe.

Sikhism's most fundamental belief is expressed in the first three words of the Mul Mantra: *Ikk Oan Kar*, "There is one Being."

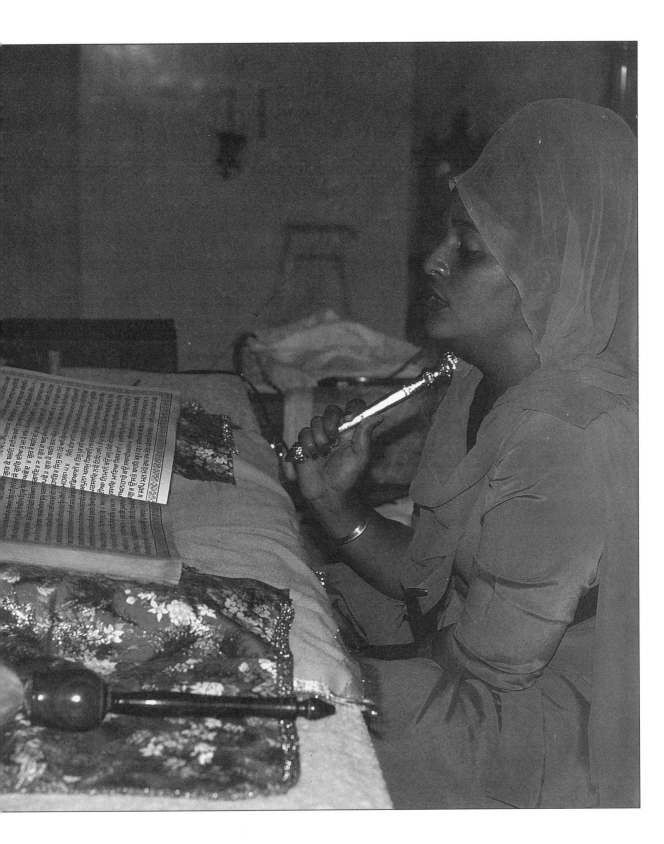

Because it is difficult to translate, many different versions exist. Here is one version:

Ikk Oan Kar	*There is one Being*
sat nam	*Truth is its name*
karta purakh	*Creator of all*
nir bhau	*Without fear*
nir vair	*Without enmity*
akal murat	*Timeless in form*
ajuni	*Unborn*
saibhang	*Self-existent*
gur prasad	*[Discovered] through the gift of the enlightener*

Ikk

The first word of the Mul Mantra is usually written as the numeral *One* and proclaims the existence and total Oneness of the Ultimate Reality. In the Mul Mantra, this Ultimate Reality is defined by what it is not: It is without human form and is genderless. It is not limited by space or time. It has no color and no shape, no beginning and no end. It fears nothing and is at odds with nothing. With these words, Sikhism rejects outright the Hindu belief in *avtarvad*, or divine incarnation, the embodiment of a god in human form. Moreover, because the Ultimate Reality has no form, it cannot be represented visually. There can be no pictures or statues of it. In fact, there is no way to portray it at all.

In focusing on the One, Sikhism rejects the many gods of Hinduism. Guru Nanak states, "In comparison with the Fearless, Formless One, innumerable gods are as dust." The One is above the traditional Hindu deities, such as Vishnu the Preserver, and Siva the Destroyer. "Millions of Vishnus has It created, millions of universes has It spawned, millions of Sivas has It raised and assimilated," says the Guru Granth.

Yet Sikh scripture wholeheartedly accepts and affirms the many ways of reaching the Singular Reality, or the One. Nanak never asked people to renounce their religions. To the contrary, he asked them to acknowledge and be whoever they were as fully as possible. Of the Hindus, he asked that they be authentic Hindus;

of the Muslims, that they be authentic Muslims. The One is common to people from all faiths and cultures.

Arjan, the fifth guru, reinforced Nanak's vision. He declared that underneath, all true religions are the same: "Some call it Rama, some call it Khuda; some worship it as Vishnu; some as Allah." By stressing the basic similarity of the Hindu and Islamic traditions, represented respectively by Rama and Khuda, Sikh gurus tried to bring peace and harmony to their divided society. To Sikhs, the differences were superficial—formalities and externals only. The Ultimate Reality is the same for all people. In the words of Guru Gobind Singh:

> . . . *Hindus and Muslims are one!*
> *The same Reality is the creator and preserver of all;*
> *Know no distinctions between them.*
> *The monastery and the mosque are the same;*
> *So are the Hindu form of worship* [puja] *and the*
>   *Muslim prayer* [namaz].
> *Humans are all one!*

This Oneness of Reality forms the bedrock of Sikhism. As a result, scholars categorize Sikhism as a monotheistic religion. Yet to term Sikhism mono-*theistic* misses an important part of Guru Nanak's vision. Sikhism does not subscribe to a belief in a majestic Theos, or personal god. The Sikh Reality is indeed One, but it has no image or form. For Nanak, the One is the experience of utter infinity: *Ikk Oan Kar*. This dimension of personal experience is central to Sikh thought.

Oan

From the rich variety of Arabic, Persian, and Sanskrit words that he might have used to express the One, Nanak chose the Punjabi word *Oan*. The Sanskrit word for the same concept, *Aum* or *Om*, means "being."

The *Mandukya Upanishad*, a Hindu scripture, explains *Aum* as a four-level journey of the mind. The first stage, *A*, is the realm of consciousness. In that stage, people are aware of the world and of their separateness from others: *I* versus *it* or *them*. The second stage, *U*, is the subconscious state in which absolute categories

> ■ *The Symbol of Sikhism*
>
> *The symbol of Sikhism, which stands for bravery and spiritual power and which flies over gurudwaras everywhere, consists of two curved swords to remind Sikhs to serve the Ultimate Reality by teaching the truth and by fighting to defend what is right, a discus, or circle, to serve as a reminder to all Sikhs that Reality is one, and in the middle, a* **khanda,** *the double-edged sword used to prepare* **amrit.**

start to break down. In that state, people experience an expansion of the mind. The logical world begins to dissolve and, transported by a higher consciousness, one might experience being in two places at the same time. The third stage, *M*, is a state of deep sleep, or total unconsciousness. It is like sleeping so soundly that one does not recall the difference between having slept for a minute or for an entire day.

In the fourth and final stage, the *A*, the *U*, and the *M* are fused. This is the experience of total unity. In this state, the self experiences a state of oneness with the Ultimate Reality. For the Sikhs, Guru Nanak's use of *Oan*, or *Aum*, expresses the belief that the Ultimate Reality is an inner experience rather than an objective knowledge of God.

Sat Nam

The second line of the Mul Mantra, *sat nam*, literally means "Truth is the Name." The first stanza of the Guru Granth's first hymn, the Jap, explains further: "Truth it has been from timeless eternity, Truth it has been within circles of temporality, Truth it is in the present, and Truth it shall be forever."

To the Sikhs, Truth is not an objective category but a way of being. Immediately after the statement on Truth, the Jap asks, "How to live a Truthful life? How to break the barriers of falsity?" The transition from Truth to true living is immediate and spontaneous. Reality is not just known objectively. It must be lived.

Other Sikh Philosophy

In its first two lines, the Mul Mantra introduces the fundamental beliefs of Sikhism. Other ideas, central to Sikh philosophy and thought but not directly stated in the Mul Mantra, follow logically from it.

Hukm is an Arabic word meaning "Divine Order," or "Divine Will." As Creator of All, the Ultimate Reality operates through it. Both creation and continuing life depend on hukm.

The beginning of the world is the outcome of hukm. Sikh philosophy claims that the genesis of the world cannot be known: "No one knows the time nor the hour, nor the date, nor the month, nor the season when creation originated . . . Through

A Sikh devotee pauses to read the **hukm,** or divine command, of the day as she enters the gurudwara.

hukm everything came to be but what the hukm is, no one can describe," says Nanak in the Jap. In accordance with hukm, the Divine Will, all of creation sprang forth in its countless varieties.

Natural cycles such as growth and death are also maintained through hukm. So is the psychological and physical makeup of human beings. Their feelings and emotions, such actions as seeing, talking, hearing, or walking, and their blessings and misfortunes all come from the Divine Will. In the Guru Granth, hukm is presented as the all-embracing principle that governs all activity. Hukm is not apart from the world. It is a link between the universe and its divine Source and Preserver.

Nadar is a Persian word, loosely translated as "grace." It is related to the Persian *nazar,* meaning "sight" or "vision." In Sikh thought, *nadar* refers to the divine glance of favor. Everyone and everything exist within in the orbit of divine vision: "All action takes place within its sight; nothing happens outside of it." The unsleeping eye of nadar on the world is a sign of the benevolent aspect of the Ultimate One. Nadar is esteemed as a precious gift.

In general, Sikhs believe that after they die, they will be reborn into the world in a new form. Their good deeds in this life can help them to achieve a better future life. But nadar, the benevolent glance, can break the cycle of death and rebirth. Instead of being born into a new body, a person can be united with the Formless One. According to the Jap, "Through actions one achieves the body, but, through the benevolent glance (nadar), one attains liberation from the cycle of birth and death." Nadar thus allows Sikhs to reach their ideal, a state of not simply knowing the Ultimate Reality, but of being one with it.

Sabad is translated as "Word." In Sikh thought, *sabad* is both the way in which the Divine is revealed and the path leading to the Divine Reality. The Guru Granth says that "The singular One has neither form nor color nor any material; but It is manifested through the true Word (Sabad)." Like reality, the Word has no substance. It cannot be seen or touched. So it is appropriate that the Word represent the formless nature of the Ultimate, which is transcendent, above all things in the physical universe.

It was through the Divine Word that Nanak's revelation at the River Bein came. He saw no Being, but he clearly heard the call. According to Sikh belief, everyone is endowed with an inner voice that speaks a Divine message. This is the *anahad sabad*, the "Soundless Word." How may the Soundless Word be heard? How may people learn to recognize the Divine within? The answer again is sabad. The so-called "Word" of the gurus clears the way so that individuals can hear the Word within themselves.

The final line of the Mul Mantra, *gur prasad*, states that Ikk Oan Kar, the One, is recognized through the grace of the guru. Again, this knowledge is not purely intellectual. Rather it is a deeply felt truth that echoes within each person. The gurus do not present an external truth. Instead, the Word evokes a harmonic response from a Truth that is already inside every individual.

Physical Images

In the Guru Granth, the gurus express the abstract concepts of Sikh philosophy in concrete images. They describe the special relationship between the Ultimate Reality and humankind in terms of intimate human relationships. "You are my father, you are my mother, you are my brother, you are my friend," says Guru Arjan. Images of conception, the growth of the unborn child in its mother's womb, and birth express the creative force of the Ultimate. "From mother's blood and father's semen is created the human form," says the Guru Granth. "In the warmth of mother's womb are we first formed."

The writers often speak from the point of view of a woman, who addresses the Formless One as "Beloved." In giving these yearnings a female voice, Sikh scripture differs from the scriptures of most other faiths, which are more male-oriented. The Sikh view is that a separation between male and female denies the wholeness of human nature. Sikh scripture emphasizes instead the significance of being human. In it, men and women share human suffering and human hope.

Marriage, the highest experience of human love, becomes a metaphor that describes the longing for the Ultimate Reality. A bride awaiting her divine groom addresses the Ultimate Reality in intimate terms: "O my handsome, unfathomable Beloved," she says. In another verse, she lavishly praises the One: "My groom is utterly glorious, brilliantly crimson, compassionate, beneficent, beloved, enticer of the hearts, overflowing with beauty like the crimson flower."

The Guru Granth uses a wide variety of images to show the many ways of connecting with the Ultimate One. These images help to make the abstract concept of the Universal Reality concrete and understandable for Sikh believers. The potter with his clay, the blacksmith with his anvil, the woman adorning herself for her loved one, the mother nursing her child, the animals of the earth, all become metaphors for the relationship of the Universal One to humankind. The explicit male and female imagery in the Guru Granth does not contradict the formless nature of the Ultimate One. Rather it suggests a vast inclusiveness. The Ultimate Reality is above all and includes all. Whatever human beings can experience in their world is a part of the Ultimate Reality. The varied imagery opens up a range of possibilities for experiencing that Ultimate One.

Form and Formless

Both physical and metaphysical qualities, form and formlessness, coexist in the Sikh conception of the Ultimate. Guru Arjan says, "Formless and Form It is both, enchanting me so!—" According to Sikh belief, the Unknowable is not completely unknown. Bits of It may be gleaned from the varied physical forms of the world. Through various hints, human mind and spirit can be launched on a voyage of discovery toward It. Guru Nanak tries to describe the One: "You have a thousand eyes but without eyes you are; you have a thousand forms but without form you are; you have a thousand feet, but without feet you are. . . ." Human language is not adequate to describe this unique One. In awe, the guru exclaims, "I am thoroughly enchanted!"

Within and Above All

The Ultimate Reality also presents a paradox, or seeming contradiction: The One is infinite, endless; yet it exists within a finite cosmos, a universe with definite limits. Many verses in the

Guru Granth signify the presence of the Ultimate Reality within the world and within all beings.

> There is a light in all and the light is That One.

> In nature It is seen, in nature heard, in nature lies
>   the essence of joy and peace
> Earth, skies and nether regions comprise nature
> The whole creation is an embodiment of It.

> You are the Primal Being, you are the Infinite Creator
> None can comprehend your limits!
> Within each and every being you are, constantly
>   pervading all.

In Sikh thought, the Ultimate Reality is transcendent, above all else. The cosmos depends on the all-knowing and all-seeing Being for its creation and preservation; but, at the same time, the Reality is present within all of its creation and is part of the fiber of all being. This suggests to some scholars of religion that the Sikh understanding of the Reality is pantheistic, the God in everything. This view, however, veers away from the sense of wonder that is at the heart of the Sikh experience of the Ultimate Reality: The One is present in all of creation, but it is never completely contained in any one thing.

At the core of Guru Nanak's awe-inspired message is the understanding that all visible forms are a part of the Formless. Western thinkers, like the Greek philosopher Plato, have tended to separate ideas and pure forms from the particular examples. In this view, only the universal idea of "rose" is real. Particular roses—those that can be seen, smelled, and touched—are changeable and temporary and, therefore, unreal. The Sikh perspective is to see the particular in the universal and the universal in the particular. Form is formless and vice versa. The Ultimate is within everything and above everything at the same time.

For Sikhs, the understanding of the Ultimate Reality is a dynamic process. They see a constant, fluid connection between the things of the world and the Ultimate. Because the Ultimate is within everything, the world is a joyous place, full of possibility and hope.

CHAPTER 5

Sikh Ethics

S ikh ethics, or code of behavior, can be summed up in Guru Nanak's words: "Truth is higher than all, but higher still is true living." The Mul Mantra named the infinite One as Truth. Nanak viewed Truth as the highest Reality. Yet his words suggest that it is not enough to know the truth. One must live it as well.

Sikhism regards human life as very precious. All forms of life are worthy of respect, but Sikhs feel that humans are especially favored because they can approach the Divine One. All humans come from the One, so all have within them a spark of the Divine. The goal of the Sikh moral code is to help people experience that divine spark within themselves.

The Problem of Haumai

If everyone has a spark of divine Truth within, what keeps people from experiencing it fully? According to Sikhism, the root cause of human suffering is *haumai*. Haumai literally means "I-myself," and it refers to egotism. Pride, arrogance, and a constant focus on "I" and "me" and "mine" separates the individual from others and from the Universal One. In the Jap, Guru Nanak

compares haumai to a wall that separates a person from the Universal Reality. An egotistical person's life is marked by competition, malice, ill will toward others, and a craving for power. Blinded by self, the person lives for himself or herself alone. Sikhs have a word to describe such a person: *man mukh*, which means "turned toward oneself." In contrast, *gur mukh*, "turned toward the guru," describes someone in harmony with the Divine Word. A person who is full of haumai never experiences the joy of the the divine spark within. Haumai is a chain holding humans in the cycle of death and life.

Overcoming Haumai

How may someone overcome haumai? As Sikhs see it, external actions like pilgrimages, fasts, and other practices of self-denial are useless. The walls of ego can be broken down, however, by following a simple formula from Guru Nanak's Jap: *sunia, mania man kita bhau*—"hearing, having faith, being full of love."

Sunia literally means "hearing." In the Jap, it means listening to the Divine Word. It is the first step on a journey toward unity with the Ultimate Reality. According to Nanak, through listening come knowledge and wisdom, and through listening all suffering and distress lose their power. The sound of the Divine Name, Truth, leads the listener to the ultimate goal: immortality and freedom from the grip of death. The refrain in the Jap repeats that those who hear the Name remain in constant bliss.

Nanak explains that human words are not adequate to explain the Ultimate Reality. However, words provide hints of Truth. They are the means of naming, praising, knowing, singing, and discussing the One. People communicate through words, and the Ultimate Reality speaks through the words of people. "As the One utters, that is how the words are arranged," the guru says. Hearing the Divine Word is the first step toward living truly.

Mania means "having faith." It is the second step on the spiritual journey. Nanak himself says that this step is hard to define. It is emotional, not intellectual, truth. Faith cannot be discussed or analyzed. However, Nanak describes the state of faith as the pathway to freedom, open to everyone. By believing in the Divine Word, Sikhs understand that they not only free

A Sikh family poses for a portrait. The family is the center of Sikh life.

themselves from the cycle of birth and death, they also help to free other members of the community, their family and friends, who are linked together by the grace of the ultimate One.

Man kita bhau means "to be full of love." This third step goes well beyond hearing the Divine Name and having faith. Love frees those who love from all limitations and barriers. It dissolves the individual ego and opens people to experiencing the other. Nanak suggests that love is the highest form of action:

> *Those who hear, appropriate and nurture love in*
> *their hearts,*
> *They cleanse themselves by bathing at the sacred*
> *fount which is within.*

Love purifies the soul. It is essential in Sikh ethics. The Guru Granth applauds love as the supreme virtue:

> *They who worship the One with adoring love and*
> *thirst for Its True Love,*
> *They who beseechingly cry out—discover peace,*
> *for in their heart lies love.*

The tenth guru, Gobind Singh, wrote of love as the pathway to the infinite One. It is a central theme in his composition, *Bacitar Natak*. "Only they who love find the Ultimate Reality," he writes. For the Sikh gurus, love is the only path to true liberation: "They who have love within their hearts alone are emancipated"—in Punjabi, *jisu antari priti lagai so mukta*.

Sikh ethics is a way of expressing love for the Ultimate One. The institutions of langar, seva, sangat, and the Khalsa provide an outlet for this love. Acts of love toward all fellow beings show love for the One. Since all are equally children of the One, they are treated like kinfolk. The response of love is vital to Sikh philosophy and ethics alike.

Popular Morality

At the everyday level, Sikh morality is best summed up in this maxim: *kirat karni, vand chhakna, te nam japna*: "to labor for one's keep, to share with others, and to practice the repetition of the Divine Name."

Kirat karni is one of the basics of Sikh ethics. In Punjabi, *kirat* means "the labor of one's hands." It is manual work—honest, upright work in pursuit of one's living. The term underscores the dignity of all labor. Sikhs understand it to mean that not to work if one is able is an offense to the faith. Honest work and its satisfactions create a positive attitude toward life. Sikhs reject withdrawal from society. Home and family are the rule.

Vand chhakna is the sharing of money and goods before using them oneself. The phrase comes from *vand*, "distribution," or "sharing," and *chhakna*, "to eat." It is based on mutual respect and sharing among equals, not on charity. Just as members of a family share their earnings and goods with one another for the good of the whole, so Sikhs try to act in the larger family of the community for its well-being. This principle of sharing is basic to the institutions of sangat and langar, which have been primary factors in shaping Sikh conduct.

Nam japna is to remember the Divine Name. *Nam* literally means "name," and *japna*, to "repeat," or "meditate on." Constantly to repeat the name of the One is a great virtue in Sikh religion. A line in the Guru Granth says nam is more important spiritually than other traditionally religious actions: "Superior to all acts of piety, charity, and austerity, is nam." Nam does not take the place of other acts, but it is the source from which all ethical action comes. According to Guru Amar Das, "Chastity, truth, continence, all are contained in nam; without contemplation on nam, one does not become pure." Sikhs remind themselves of nam throughout the day by repeating the guru mantra, *Wahe Guru,*" which means "Wonderful Guru," or "God is great."

The Path to Ultimate Reality

In the final lines of the Jap, Guru Nanak presents five stages by which human beings can ascend toward the Ultimate Reality. They are a path leading to higher and higher levels of experience. They are the realms, or regions, of duty, knowledge, art, grace, and truth and can be described as follows:

Dharam Khand: The first stage is *Dharam Khand,* the realm of duty. This is the earthly life. It is made up of nights and seasons and dates and days, of time and space. The world contains uncounted varieties of life. "Within this infinite matrix are myriads of species, infinite are their names and forms," says Nanak. Through the Ultimate Reality, all are interconnected, and people should live harmoniously with them. Being on earth offers people the opportunity to live ethically and with purpose. Earthly existence is not to be scorned, but to be lived fully and intensely. Sikhs believe that actions are important, for whatever someone does has an effect. While on earth, it is the duty of all people to put their ethical standards into practice.

Gyan Khand: The second stage is *Gyan Khand,* the realm of knowledge. Here the individual becomes aware of the vastness of creation: millions of inhabited planets like our Earth, countless mountains, countless moons, suns, and constellations. When someone realizes how limitless creation is, he or she also realizes how small human beings are. Knowledge of creation brings with it an awe of the creator. Humility replaces ego. Knowledge destroys limitations and prejudices and creates an all-accepting and all-welcoming attitude.

Saram Khand: The third stage, *Saram Khand,* is the realm of art. Art sharpens and refines human sensibility. In this realm,

Sikh children at an informal "Sunday school" read and listen to stories of the gurus and learn about their faith.

people develop an appreciation of beauty. It is an important stage in the spiritual journey. In Nanak's words, "One who can appreciate fragrance will alone know the flower." Unless they can feel the power of beauty, people cannot know the Ultimate Reality, which is there to see, hear, taste, touch, and smell in this world. Sikhs do not distinguish between physical, mental, and spiritual senses. A person has all of these. As Nanak says, "Here are sharpened consciousness, wisdom, mind, and discrimination." The cultivation of the appreciation of beauty opens the way to the next stage of spiritual development.

Karam Khand: The fourth stage, *Karam Khand,* is the realm of grace. Nanak describes it as the home of those who love the One. "Here live warriors and heroes of mighty power," he says. Who are these warriors and heroes? "The true hero," says Nanak, "is one who kills the evil of egotism within." Physical strength and power are not the ideal. Sikhs say, "by conquering oneself, one conquers the world." Indeed, they see outer conquests as being much easier than internal ones. Heroines and heroes in this realm of grace are those who are in control of themselves. They are exempt from the cycle of birth and death. "They are rejoicing, for that True One is close to their hearts," says the guru. Firm in their conviction and full of joy, they ascend to the final stage in their quest for the Ultimate Reality.

Sach Khand: The realm of truth, *Sach Khand*, is the fifth and highest stage. The opening of the Guru Granth names the One, *Ikk Oan Kar*, as "Truth." The realm of truth is the sphere of the One, the home of the Ultimate Reality. In the home of the Ultimate Reality the individual and the Divine One merge. The benevolent glance of the One and the joyful vision of those who seek it come together. Nanak describes this stage as "hard as iron." It cannot be expressed in human terms, except as union with infinity. "Here are continents, constellations, and universes, their counting never ending, never. . . ." For the individual there will be no more rebirths into the world, and no more lives, and no more deaths. The self is freed from all limitations of space, time, gender, and earthly considerations. They are replaced by absolute joy. "Truth is higher than all, but higher still is true living," says the guru. In *Sach Khand*, the individual finally reaches true living. It is the purpose of all human existence.

The Sikh spiritual journey is one of love for fellow beings, the experience of life in the world, and an insight into beauty. It is not a journey away from the world. Rather it is grounded in life on earth. It is on earth that Sikhs work to develop their moral, intellectual, artistic, and spiritual capacities and to catch a glimpse of the Ultimate Reality. The higher they ascend, the more deeply they feel that they experience life here and now.

CHAPTER **6**

Religious Life
and Rites
of Passage

W hether they live in a traditional community in a Punjabi village or in an ultra-modern suburb of Los Angeles or Chicago, Sikhs attempt to connect their every daily activity to their religion.

Religious Life

A Sikh's first words of greeting reveal the deeply religious dimension of his or her life. When one Sikh meets another, each greets the other by placing his or her two hands together, gently bowing, and saying, *Sat Sri Akal*, which means "Truth is the Timeless One." Their greeting is quite different from the usual Western greeting of shaking hands and calling each other by name. The Sikh greeting combines the second line of the Mul Mantra, "Truth is the Name," and the ideal of Sikh ethics, the last stage of spiritual ascension, unity with the formless One. Instead of speaking their own names as they greet one another, Sikhs humbly acknowledge the One as their True Reality.

The Sikhs' appearance is noticeably different. Men and teenage boys do not shave their beards or cut their hair. Men and

*Preceding page-
In their gurudwara,
Sikh women celebrate
Baisakhi, the New Year,
by singing hymns from
the Guru Granth and
playing traditional
instruments.*

young boys wear the turban, which is made from almost five yards of cloth and comes in many colors. Little boys wear their hair coiled in a topknot with a kerchief tied around it. Male athletes also wear the topknot, since sprinting or other such activities would be difficult to do while wearing a turban. Uncut hair is one of the Five Ks, symbols of the Khalsa, established by Guru Gobind Singh in the seventeenth century.

*A father and son
display Sikh headgear.
The father wears the
turban, and the boy
wears his uncut hair in
a topknot covered by a
scarf, the traditional style
of Sikh youngsters.*

Women and girls refrain from cutting their hair as well. Young girls wear long braids, and women tie up their hair in a variety of styles. Sikh women dress in a particular style and they can be identified by their clothing—loose trousers called *salvars*, a shirt that reaches to the knees, and a long, sheer scarf wound around the neck or over the head.

On festive occasions, the colors of the Sikhs' turbans and scarves are usually quite brilliant. On serious occasions, the headgear is usually more somber. Both men and women wear a steel bracelet around the right wrist. The steel of the bracelet symbolizes spiritual courage and strength, and the circle is a reminder of the unity of the Ultimate One, which has no beginning and no end.

Finally, the Sikh surnames, Singh for men and Kaur for women, reflect their religion, proclaiming membership in a society of equals and marking them as Sikhs. Sikhs consider all members of the Sikh community to be part of their extended family. Sikhs refer to friends and even distant associates as family members. Parents' friends and associates are referred to as "uncles" and "aunts." Children accept the friends of their brothers and sisters as their own brothers and sisters and the friends of their parents and grandparents as their own parents and grandparents. Until recent times, a Punjabi village was regarded as a family unit, and people from the same village were not permitted to marry because the relationship was too close. Throughout their lives, Sikhs try to bring others into their own family, breaking down the barriers of caste, race, and religion.

Sikhs weave their religion into their lives. They try to incorporate the spirit of seva and langar into all their relationships. Sikhs enthusiastically give time and energy to family members, relatives, and friends. Complete strangers who identify themselves as coming from the same village, or as having attended the same school or college, or even as being acquainted with a relative's friend will automatically be showered with hospitality. In small areas of northern India, hotels and inns are practically unknown. Sikh guests, whether invited or not, receive a warm welcome from their host families and are given bedding and food. Seva, serving others with a cheerful attitude, is thus a part of everyday life. Sikhs seek jobs for, provide financial assistance to, and extend domestic comfort to fellow Sikhs.

In India, baby-sitting is unknown among the Sikhs. Grandparents, aunts, and uncles—whether related by blood or by faith—care for children. Even in such American cities as Los Angeles or Washington, D.C., working parents call on relatives and grandparents from the Punjab to help care for children.

Sikhs who have migrated continue to share their earnings with relatives and friends and their community, though they may

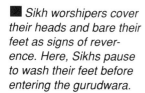
■ Sikh worshipers cover their heads and bare their feet as signs of reverence. Here, Sikhs pause to wash their feet before entering the gurudwara.

be thousands of miles away. They send money home to India for aged parents, for weddings of siblings, for schools and hospitals; in their new home, they give to charity and share their Thanksgiving meal with the homeless.

Sikhs attempt at all times to integrate the sacred with the secular. They may say their prayers alone, with their families, or with the sangat, or congregation, in the gurudwara. Morning prayers reverberate through a Sikh home as family members go about their activities. Mothers recite stanzas from the Jap as they prepare breakfast or comb their children's hair. Fathers pray while picking up bedding, cleaning, or gardening. If their home is large enough for a separate worship room, a family may gather there in the morning to recite their prayers. Some Sikhs might visit a neighborhood gurudwara, thus combining devotions with a morning walk. Others might pray as they drive to work, listen to tapes of scriptural readings, or tune their radios to a Sikh station.

Similarly, Sikhs might recite their evening prayers as they tend to various chores or relax on a bicycle ride or a walk. Others might pray in a quiet spot at home or go to the gurudwara. Some Sikhs might choose to read the Guru Granth. During certain hours of the day, Sikhs who live near a gurudwara can hear the prayers and participate from their own lawns or verandas. In the Punjab, *Kirtan*, or sacred music, is broadcast by radio and television from the Golden Temple in Amritsar, and neighbors often gather to listen to the hymns.

True living for Sikhs involves remembering the One Reality as often and as intimately as possible. The Ultimate Reality is part of time and space. Why should that One not be remembered everywhere and at every moment? From the Sikh perspective, daily routine is filled with the Divine Presence. Throughout the course of their daily schedules, Sikhs never stop expressing their love for the Divine. *Wahe Guru*—"Wonderful Guru"—the Sikhs exclaim, before and after meals, before and after anything they undertake.

Daily Prayers

Sikhs regularly recite morning prayers called *Bani*. These "five verses" are *Jap, Jaap, Swayyai, Benati Chaupai,* and *Anand,*

and they lead the worshiper through the five *khands*, the stages of spiritual development from earthly duty to heavenly bliss. With the meditation on the name of the Ultimate, the five verses form the *Nit Nem*, "the everyday routine." Every morning, as they prepare for work and school, Sikh family members ask one another, "Have you done your nit nem?" In addition, Sikhs recite two evening prayers, *Rahiras* and *Kirtan Sohila*. Before they begin their prayers, Sikhs quiet their minds by repeating the Mul Mantra five times and the guru mantra, "Wahe Guru," over and over as they meditate on the Ultimate. They also repeat the guru mantra many times throughout the day, fulfilling the commandment given to Nanak at the River Bein: "Rejoice in My Name."

Jap (pronounced JUP) is Guru Nanak's composition. It is the first prayer in the Guru Granth, and it expresses the basic philosophy of the Sikhs. Sikhs recite it at dawn, when their minds are fresh and the atmosphere is serene. The Jap describes dawn as the "ambrosial hour," or the "hour of heavenly nectar," and Sikhs feel that it is the best time for hearing the Divine Word.

Jaap (pronounced JAP) and *Swayyai* are compositions of the tenth guru, Gobind Singh. They appear in his book of poetic compositions called the *Dasam Granth*. The *Dasam Granth* is different from the Guru Granth, but Sikhs esteem it highly as the work of Gobind Singh. The Jaap and the Swayyai form an important part of their daily prayers. Jaap is a poetic offering to the Ultimate Reality. It expresses Gobind Singh's reverence for the transcendent One, and praises the One's many divine qualities. The poem is 199 couplets long. In ending with couplet 199 instead of 200, it shows that in the Ultimate, there is no ending. The Jaap has an energetic sound and rapid rhythm. Repeating it helps Sikhs to focus on the Ultimate Reality described in Nanak's Jap, and sets the tone for the day.

Swayyai are quatrains, or four-line rhymes. The ten Swayyai that Sikhs include in their daily prayers come also from the *Dasam Granth*. These rhymes stress devotion as the essence of religion. They reject all forms of external worship and express Nanak's message of love. Sikhs also recite the Swayyai during the Amrit ceremony, or baptism into the Khalsa and the fellowship of the Sikhs.

Benati Chaupai, or "supplication in quatrains" by Gobind Singh begs the help and protection of the Universal One. With the words, "I beg that I keep remembering you," Sikhs ask never to be allowed to forget the name of the Ultimate. They also ask that they be saved from evil and that their people be happy and free.

Anand, or "bliss," by Guru Amar Das, represents the end of the spiritual journey. It expresses the hope for union with the One and for the joy of being forever in the realm of truth. Before they begin their prayers, Sikhs quiet their minds by repeating the Mul Mantra five times and the Guru Mantra "Wahe Guru," over and over as they meditate on the Ultimate. They also repeat the Guru Mantra many times throughout the day, fulfilling the commandment received by Guru Nanak: "Rejoice in My Name."

Rahiras is part of the evening service. It consists of hymns from Guru Nanak, Guru Ram Das, and Guru Arjan. The Benati Chaupai is also a part of this evening prayer. The Rahiras ends with stanzas from the Anand. Summer and winter, Sikhs recite Rahiras at dusk, just as the day and the night come together. Through the Rahiras, the Sikhs show their respect to the transcendent Reality. They sing the praises of the Divine, seek the protection of the all-powerful One, and express their joy at hearing the Word within themselves.

Kirtan Sohila, "the hymn of praise," consists of five hymns and is the ending to evening prayers. Sikhs recite it as the holy book is closed before they go to bed. It is also recited at cremations, or funerals. The first three hymns are by Guru Nanak. They are followed by one each from Guru Ram Das and Guru Arjan. The first hymn speaks of the union of the individual self with the Ultimate Reality. The second presents the oneness of the Ultimate, in spite of the great diversity of scriptures, teachers, and philosophies in the world. The third rejects external piety and ritual. It portrays the cosmos worshiping in harmony—the skies, sun, moon, and stars, and all growing things are an offering to the Divine. The fourth hymn, by Ram Das, explains how the sound of the Divine Name eases all suffering and ends the cycle of death and birth. The fifth hymn, by Arjan, celebrates life on earth. It invites people to take the opportunity of life to serve others and win merit. It promises that the person who comes to know the

Divine Mystery will enjoy the bliss and freedom of spiritual immortality.

The Bhog Ceremony

The word *bhog* literally means "pleasure." It is similar to the Greek word *eucharist,* which means "thanksgiving" and, in the spiritual sense, refers to the Christian sacrament of Holy Communion. Bhog involves reading the concluding pages of the Guru Granth and sharing the Sikh sacrament of *Karahprasad,* which concludes every religious ceremony.

Bhog can take place anywhere—in a room in someone's home, in a public hall, or in a gurudwara. Its leaders are members of the Sikh congregation—Sikhism has no priests or ministers—and both men and women may lead. People gather around the Guru Granth and, usually, everyone sits on the floor, facing the holy text. Members of the community prepare Karahprasad, the sweet sacrament, which consists of equal parts of butter, flour, and sugar prepared in a large steel pot over a wood fire or on a coal, electric, or gas burner. During its preparation, Sikhs remain in an attitude of reverence, with their heads covered and their feet bare, and they recite hymns from the Guru Granth. When the Karahprasad is ready, it is put in a large, flat dish and covered with a clean cloth. Then one of the leaders respectfully lifts it and carries it on his or her head to the congregation. The steaming Karahprasad, with its rich aroma, is placed on the right side of the Guru Granth.

During bhog, a group of musicians usually sings hymns from the Guru Granth. A reader reads the inaugural hymn and then slowly begins to chant the last five pages of the Guru Granth. These pages begin with fifty-seven couplets by the ninth guru, Tegh Bahadur, and are followed by the *Mundavani,* the seal of Guru Arjan, which stamps the Guru Granth as a platter holding the three important delicacies of Truth, Contentment, and Contemplation. All who are present are invited to partake of and savor the sacrament.

After the reading, the entire congregation stands. With hands folded and heads bowed, they recite the ardas, the prayer of supplication. In this prayer, Sikhs remember the Ultimate Reality.

They recall their first ten gurus and the embodiment of their spirit in the Guru Granth. They also remember events of Sikh heroism, devotion, and martyrdom. The leading member of the gathering, or any other person who can read the *Gurmukhi* script of the Guru Granth, begins the ardas, and the congregation joins in, exclaiming, *Wahe Guru,* "Wonderful Guru."

Toward the end of the ardas, the leader asks the congregation for a special blessing. Each reading of the Guru Granth is undertaken for a special purpose, and the blessing of the day recalls that purpose. The ardas ends with the whole congregation praying for the prosperity and happiness of all humanity. While wishing for the good of all, the Sikhs bow in front of their sacred text, touching their foreheads to the ground, and then seat themselves on the floor in front of their holy book.

■ *Musicians called* **ragis** *accompany the singing of* **kirtan,** *the Sikh sacred hymns, on the* **harmonium,** *a kind of small organ, and the* **tabla,** *or drums.*

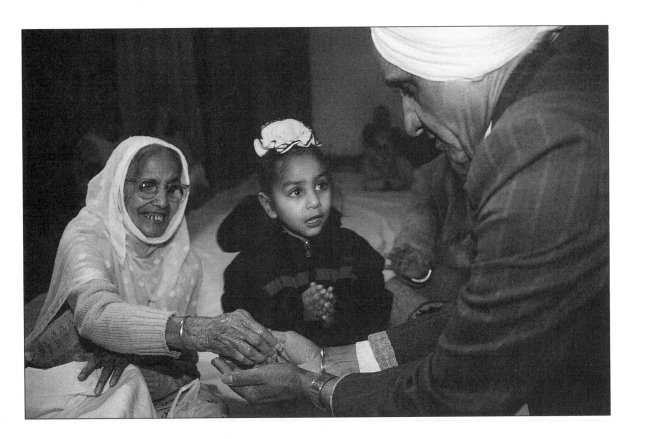

■ *Members of the congregation receive* **karahprasad,** *the Sikh sacrament.*

Then the reader opens the Guru Granth and reads the hymn at the top of the left-hand page to obtain the hukm, or Divine Command, for the day. The congregation then interprets the passage chosen from in the Guru Granth in the context of the special purpose of the day's service.

Finally, the distribution of Karahprasad takes place. Each member of the congregation receives a warm, buttery handful of the Sikh sacrament in his or her outstretched palms. The sacrament is distributed to all, regardless of religious affiliation. Many times, langar follows the bhog ceremony. The members of the congregation stand, bow before the Guru Granth, and walk outside to the lawn or into another room where langar is being served. Some seat themselves in long rows on the floor to partake of the meal, while others help with the cooking, serving, and cleaning up.

Rites of Passage

The Guru Granth is read for all rites of passage, for any family event, or for blessings on a new job or house. The readings differ: they may be continuous for forty-eight hours, or they may be any slower variation thereof. And all Sikh ceremonies culminate with the bhog ceremony. The prescribed forms for Sikh rituals relating to baptism, marriage, and death appear in the *Sikh Rahit Maryada,* or "Book of Ethical Codes." Some of the rituals are described here.

Name-Giving

In Sikhism, there are no taboos surrounding childbirth. Guru Nanak and his successors rejected the generally accepted notion in the India of their day that a household was impure, or unclean, for forty days after the birth of a child. (In traditional India, the home in which a girl was born was considered impure longer than the home in which a boy was born.) But the Sikh gurus opposed such views. They regarded the birth of any child, boy or girl, as a divine gift.

Parents take their baby for its first visit to the gurudwara as soon as such a visit is suitable. During their visit, the family offers money and silk coverings for the Guru Granth. Sometimes the family requests that the Guru Granth be fully read during the baby's first visit. Devout families often request that the baby be baptized in the Amrit ceremony, and the person performing the ceremony prepares the amrit by mixing sugar with water and reading five stanzas of the Jap. The ceremony concludes with the following prayer:

> *I present this child and with Your Grace*
> *I administer the Amrit*
> *May the child grow up to be a true Sikh*
> *Devoting the self to the service of others and the Motherland.*
> *May the child be inspired with devotion,*
> *May the holy food be acceptable to the Guru*
> *By the ever increasing glory of the Divine Name*
> *May the whole creation be blessed.*

After the prayer, a few drops of amrit are placed in the child's mouth. The mother drinks the rest of the amrit.

A Sikh couple present their baby at a name-giving ceremony.

The timing and organization of the name-giving ceremony depend on the wishes of the parents. They choose a name by consulting the Guru Granth. While the spine of the Guru Granth rests on the cushions, a reader holds the holy book closed with both hands and then gently lets open at random. The child receives a name beginning with the first letter at the top of the left-hand page of the Guru Granth. Sikhs do not often have different first names for boys and girls. The addition of the name Kaur or Singh indicates the gender of the child. The child also receives its first kara, or steel bracelet.

Musicians recite hymns of thanksgiving. A popular hymn for name-giving ceremonies contains these words: "May you have the felicitations of your father and mother and may you always remember the name of the Ultimate Provider." After the hymns, ardas is said and Karahprasad is distributed to all.

Although the birth of a child is a major event, birthday parties in Sikh life are usually quiet family affairs. Families celebrate by reciting kirtan, reading from the Guru Granth, and preparing langar. Wealthy families, however, may have big gatherings for children, almost like wedding celebrations.

Amrit Initiation

Amrit initiation is the reenactment of the ceremony that took place when the Khalsa was established by Guru Gobind Singh in 1699. *Amrit* is a Sanskrit word meaning "immortal," and it traditionally describes the nectar for immortality. In Sikhism, however, amrit is not some magical potion that leads to immortality. Rather it signifies an inner experience of Ultimate Oneness. For the Sikh initiation ceremony, amrit is prepared by mixing water and sugar with a double-edged sword while prayers are chanted. Amrit combines clarity of mind, represented by water; sweetness of character, represented by sugar; military valor, represented by the sword; and a poetic spirituality, represented by the chanting of the sacred verses. The divine nectar introduces the individual into the Khalsa, the casteless society with its belief in the One Infinite Reality.

Amrit initiation is open to all. "Any man or woman of whatever nationality, race, or social standing, who is prepared to accept the rules governing the Sikh community, has the right to receive amrit initiation," says the *Sikh Rahit Maryada*. No particular age is prescribed for initiation. It may be as soon as a boy or a girl is old enough to be able to read the scripture and comprehend the articles of the Sikh faith. Or it may be later in life—some people even wait until their own children are grown.

As with all Sikh ceremonies, the amrit initiation does not have to take place in the gurudwara. It may be conducted virtually anywhere, but it is usually held in a quiet, enclosed room. The Guru Granth and a reader must be present. Any five Sikhs who are already members of the Khalsa can administer the ceremony. The five fill a steel bowl with clean water and sugar, kneel on the right knee as if ready for battle, and recite the *Jap, Jaap, Swayyai, Chaupai,* and *Anand*. As they recite these five prayers, the five stir the water and sugar with a small sword. After the prayers, one of the five says the ardas. Then the amrit is served. The five drink the amrit from their cupped hands and sprinkle some on their eyes and hair. The initiates receive the holy liquid five times, each time saying, *Wahe guru ji ka khalsa wahe guru ji ki fateh,* "The Khalsa belongs to the Wonderful Guru and victory belongs to the Wonderful Guru."

After the ceremony, they all share the ambrosial nectar, all sipping from the same bowl. Then together they recite Guru Nanak's Mul Mantra and the guru mantra, "Wahe Guru," remembering the One Singular Reality. The initiates are told that they are now children of Guru Gobind Singh and his wife Mata Sahib Kaur. Their historical and spiritual parentage makes them all brothers and sisters, and they are to live as Khalsa Sikhs. Thus, they are to maintain the principles of the Guru Granth and their physical identity through the Five Ks. They are not to eat the meat of an animal slaughtered according to the Islamic or Kosher rituals, which Sikhs believe are painful for the animal; they may eat the meat from an animal slaughtered with one quick stroke. The distinctive Sikh rite of amrit initiation concludes with Karahprasad.

Marriage

Marriage is regarded as an important rite of passage in every society, but for the Sikhs, it is a means of serving the Divine Reality and fellow humanity. Sikhs feel that people best fulfill their individual potential within marriage. All Sikh gurus—with the exception of Guru Har Krishan, who had a short life—were married. Marriage between children, once a common practice in India, is forbidden. Divorce is legal, and both men and women can remarry. Remarriage of widows is an accepted practice as well.

Like those of most Indian couples, Sikh marriages, both in India and in Western countries, are arranged, usually by the couple's parents. Marriage arrangements may be made anytime after a young person turns eighteen; often families wait until a prospective bride or groom has finished college or become established in a career. If the couple are from the same locality, they may know each other, but this is often not the case. Sikhs see marriage not only as the uniting of two people but also as the uniting of two families, and the marriage takes place with the advice and assistance of the extended family on both sides.

Engagement

Many Sikhs weave customs into their wedding celebrations that are not specifically part of the Sikh religion but rather are a part of Punjabi culture. A formal engagement is not necessary in Sikh life, but if the two parties wish it, the engagement takes place in the presence of the Guru Granth in the future groom's house. The ceremony is thus quite different from a simple exchange of rings between the couple. In the Sikh engagement, the prospective groom and bride do not meet; the bride's relatives and friends take gifts of sweet foods, dried fruits, money, a bracelet (kara), and sometimes a ring, to the home of the groom. When the bride's group arrives, the groom's family takes them to the Guru Granth, and they place their gifts in front of the book. The two families sing scriptural hymns together, and the bride's father then presents their gifts to the prospective groom, who takes a bit of the dried fruit (*chhuhara*, or date), signifying acceptance of the match and the gifts. The families then wave money around the groom's head to symbolize a prosperous life. Later, the money is given to charity. The ceremony concludes with the recitation of the ardas and the taking of hukm.

This ceremony is often followed by one in the bride's home, in which the groom's family offers a *chunni charauna,* or red head scarf, to the bride-to-be, accompanied by jewelry, clothes, sweet foods, and other gifts, including a red thread to be braided into the bride's hair. The red head scarf is to be worn by the bride at the engagement ceremony. To people in the East, red is the color of good fortune. The sign of blood and life, red is the color of the Sikh bridal outfit. During the engagement, the bride, with her female relatives, has her own celebration with her female relatives, who paint her hands with henna and sing songs and dance together.

One to three days prior to the wedding, the prospective bride and the groom observe separate periods of seclusion. Both avoid dressing up and going out, but their homes resound with joy and music. In the evenings female friends and relatives on both sides gather and sing songs to the accompaniment of a drum. While the lead singer plays the drum placed beneath her knee, her companion beats on the wooden center with a spoon, and the others sing Punjabi folk songs. The songs on the groom's side are called *ghorian*, and those on the bride's side are called *suhag*. The singers may make up songs on the spot. Often a team of young girls completes against a team of older women, and the competition is vigorous.

On the eve of the wedding, both bride and groom take ritual baths in their respective homes. Each is given a massage with a mixture of flour, turmeric, and milk. A traditional version of a modern bath scrub, the mixture leaves the skin light and clean. This rite of purification is accompanied by song, music, and clapping. After the bath, each puts on new clothes. From her maternal relatives, the bride receives a head band, a nose-ring, ivory bracelets, clothes, and utensils. The bride's family also provides new outfits for the groom and his family.

Sihra Bandhi

Before the groom and his party leave for the marriage ceremony at the bride's home, they observe several rituals. First, they recite the ardas. Then comes *sihra bandhi,* a ceremony in which the eldest sister ties a *sihra,* a shining veil made of gilded strings with a plume on top, around the groom's forehead. In return for this tying, or *bandhi,* the sister receives money from the groom. Then the groom's eldest sister-in-law (his brother's wife) puts kohl—a dark cosmeticlike eye shadow—around the groom's eyes. In the meantime, the mare on which the groom will travel to the bride's home is fed with barley and *gram,* a flour mixture. The sister decorates the mare and braids her reins with red thread. Just as everything is complete and the groom is ready to proceed, the groom's sister takes the reins of the horse and jokingly demands gifts from her brother, and the groom gives money to his sisters and cousins. A younger brother or a nephew or cousin of the groom acts as the best man, and as the procession begins, he sits behind the groom on the horse.

Milni

When they reach the bride's home, a formal meeting of the two families takes place. This meeting is called *milni.* The bride's party receives the groom's party by chanting hymns of welcome. Ardas is said. Introductions follow. The father of the groom is introduced to the father of the bride, the mother to the mother, brother to brother, uncle to uncle, and friend to friend. Each family member meets the other with a welcoming embrace. Often, members of the bride's family give gifts such as blankets and jewelry to the family of the groom. Once again, the members of the wedding party wave money around one another's heads. Then the wedding group makes its way toward the Guru Granth.

Anand Karaj

The Sikh marriage ceremony is known as *Anand Karaj*, which literally means "blissful occasion," and in which the groom and bride circle the Guru Granth four times as the wedding hymns are chanted. This is a legal ceremony as well as a religious one. It was officially recognized as such by the Sikh Marriage Act of 1909. Anand Karaj can be traced back to the time of the third guru, Amar Das, who is the author of the forty-stanza hymn called *Anand*. Six stanzas from this hymn form a part of the Sikhs' daily prayers, and the complete Anand is recited on all important occasions. The *Lavan*, meaning "circling," a hymn in four stanzas, was composed by the fourth guru, Ram Das, and is also part of the Sikh wedding ceremony.

The Anand Karaj can take place in a gurudwara or at home on a terrace, in a courtyard, in a drawing room—anywhere, so long as the Guru Granth is present. The ceremony begins with the singing of scriptural hymns. While kirtan, the musical recitations, are going on, the guests and hosts assemble. After bowing, the groom sits down before the holy book. The bride, accompanied by her friends and relatives, joins him and sits on his left. The opening ardas is said. This time, with the exception of the couple and their respective parents or guardians, the entire congregation is seated. Blessings are sought for the couple. Musicians sing a passage from the Guru Granth recounting how one rejoices and tastes nectar in the company of saints.

A scholar or a politician next makes a formal speech, addressing the couple and explaining the significance of Sikh marriage. The speaker reminds the couple of their obligations, not only toward each other but also toward their families, their community, and society at large. Usually the speaker reiterates Guru Amar Das's emphasis on marriage as a "union of the divine spark" rather than as a civil or social contract. In the Guru Granth, the fourth guru says, "They are not husband and wife who sit side by side next to each other; only they are truly wedded who personify one single spirit in two bodies."

After the speech, the bride's father unites the bride and groom with a saffron-colored scarf. He places one end of the scarf in the groom's hands, passes it over the groom's shoulder, and places the other end in the bride's hand. The musicians recite a scriptural verse that urges the bride to ignore all empty praise and slander and be totally attached to the bond symbolized by the scarf. This rite of linking the couple together is a physical representation of the spiritual union mentioned in the Guru Granth. Tied with the scarf, husband and wife, together, are to renounce all evil and devote themselves fully to the Ultimate Reality. However, many take this rite to mean that the daughter is no longer a part of her parents' family and henceforth belongs entirely to her husband and her husband's family. It is a solemn moment.

The actual marriage ceremony begins with the opening of the Guru Granth and the reading of the Lavan, which describes marriage as a rite of passage into higher and higher circles of existence. As each verse is recited and sung, the couple reverentially circle the Guru Granth in a clockwise direction. To show their support, relatives help the couple as they circuit the holy book. During the fourth stanza, the entire congregation showers the bride and groom with flower petals as a sign of rejoicing. The ceremony concludes with the customary singing of passages from Anand and the recitation of ardas, this time with the entire congregation standing. Finally, hukm, the divine command, is received from the Guru Granth, and Karahprasad, the sweet sacrament, is served to the entire congregation.

In different parts of the world, Sikhs have adopted a variety of ceremonies. But essentially, the religious ceremony is simple, consisting of circling the Guru Granth four times. Before and after each circuit, the couple bows before the Guru Granth. This gesture is symbolic of their marriage consent and their commitment to each other. No vows are exchanged, no kisses are given, no legal materials are signed or witnessed. The four circlings and the recitations of the Lavan constitute the Sikh marriage, a marriage that is both religious and legal.

Doli

The marriage ceremony is followed by a festive lunch. But the joyous mood soon changes to one of sadness: the bride must leave her parents' home. Amidst farewell songs and tears, the bride departs with the groom's party to his home. Her departure is called *doli*, which refers to the traditional marriage procession of India in which the bride was carried on a *palanquin*, a covered seat atop two poles. Today, the means of transportation varies from horse carts to decorated limousines. Relatives and friends greet the bride at the other end, and then many other rites are performed, such as pouring oil on the threshold, circulating a bowl of water around the couple's heads, and eating rice and grains. In modern families, the groom's family gives a reception, and the couple cuts the wedding cake.

Death

In Sikhism, life and death are regarded as natural processes. According to the Guru Granth, just as each day that dawns must reach its end, so must all people depart. For Sikhs, death does not mean an absolute end. The Sikh gurus and their scripture stress the moral, intellectual, and spiritual refinement of the individual; their concern is with development here and now. The Sikh ideal is to attain infinity and immortality; the objective is to become part of the Ultimate Reality. As a result, when the physical, finite existence ends, it is not viewed as a final terminating point.

Sikhs believe that when a person is about to die, his or her attention is drawn toward the Ultimate. No worldly sorrows or grief should intrude on the peaceful departure. External signs of grief, such as weeping, wailing, or beating one's breasts and thighs, which are quite common in northern India, are forbidden in Sikh life. Sikh life is intergenerational, with young couples, their children, parents, and grandparents often living under one roof. The elderly are not consigned to homes for the aged; they grow old and die at home. Thus, even the youngest Sikh children become familiar with death, and as adults, they accept death more matter-of-factly than do many people in the West, where death occurs mostly in hospitals and nursing homes.

When someone dies early in life or from some unnatural cause, people demonstrate their grief. But when the elderly die—

Guru Hargobind was imprisoned by officers of Emperor Jahangir for nonpayment of fines imposed on his father. Furthermore, his raising of an army had put him under suspicion of treason. But after examining the case, the emperor decided to release the guru.

With the Sikh guru in prison were fifty-two Hindu princes, and the guru refused to leave unless his Hindu companions were set free also. According to tradition, the emperor agreed, but on one condition. Only those princes could leave who could pass through a narrow passageway without losing hold of the guru's garments. Not to be outdone, the guru ordered a cloak for himself, made with long tassels hanging from it. The impossible was made possible: holding on to the tassels, all fifty-two princes walked to freedom.

At the Golden Temple, Sikhs celebrate Divali for three days. Electric lights and earthenware oil lamps illuminate the central shrine, the walkways, and the adjoining building. Candles and lanterns float in the surrounding pool. Reflections of the temple lights merge with the floating lamps in a shimmering display. Fireworks light the night sky. Singers and musicians perform kirtan, the Sikh sacred music. Speakers deliver lectures and recite heroic ballads. Sikhs offer gifts of cash, flowers, Karahprasad, rice, butter, milk, and flour. Crowds come to view the Golden Temple's collection of precious jewels and to marvel at the golden gates, the golden canopy with its bejeweled peacock, the pearl tassels, the golden fans, and the fly whisk made from millions of hairlike sandalwood fibers.

During Divali, people whitewash and paint their homes and decorate them with earthenware lamps and candles. Families and friends exchange gifts and candy. For the Sikhs at this time, as for Hindus, Christians, and Jews around the world, the lights symbolize peace and joy.

Hola Mohalla

Holi is a traditional spring festival of the Hindus. It celebrates the playful presence of their dark god, Lord Krishna. The festival occurs just as winter mellows into spring. During the Holi celebration, people throw brightly colored paint and dye on one another. Friends and strangers alike are sprayed, splashed, and especially those who have lived a long and happy life, witnessing the birth of children and grandchildren—grief is muted. Death is presumed to be a stage that completes the liberation of the soul, and Sikhs sing praises to the Ultimate. The body is carried in a procession with musicians playing and singing, a ritual that is reminiscent of the bridegroom going to wed his bride.

The Sikhs cremate their dead. Guru Nanak himself was not concerned with whether his body would be cremated or buried or floated down the river, so his followers adopted cremation for practical reasons. Since Sikhs believe that the body is made up of four elements and that during cremation it returns to the four elements, cremation also seems to be more natural. Fire merges with the fire that is lighted; the earth goes to the earth, the air to the air, and the bones (called *phul*, literally, "flowers") are immersed in running water, signifying the return of the fourth element to water itself.

When a person dies, the body is bathed and dressed in clean clothes. A young woman is often dressed in her bridal clothes. We thus find another connection between death and marriage. The body is covered with white sheets, placed on a bier, or platform, and carried to the cremation ground on the shoulders of four people closest to the deceased. As the funeral procession moves, mourners recite passages from the Guru Granth and sing the following hymn:

> *Wake up my mind, wake up from the oblivion of sleep*
> *The body that came with you will soon bid you goodbye . . .*
> *Says Nanak, sing the praise of the Ultimate One*
> *For all else is an ephemeral dream. . . .*

Even during one's last journey on earth, the Sikh is called on to recognize and praise the Eternal Reality.

When the mourners reach the cremation ground, they place the body on a platform of firewood. A close relative lights the funeral pyre and then those present recite the evening hymn, Kirtan Sohila. The wedding symbol pervades this daily prayer of the Sikhs:

> *The day of my wedding is fixed,*
> *In unison, O friends, pour ritual oil.*

Bless me that I unite with my Groom.
From home to home these summons are received daily
Remember the Summoner, O friends,
  for this day must come to one and all.

A funeral is a rite of passage, just as a marriage ceremony is. The oil of blessing is poured out in both rituals. This scriptural verse attempts to overcome the fear of death. It presents death as something all share and as a passage that opens people into a union with the Transcendent Reality. Following the Kirtan Sohilia, ardas is offered, seeking blessing for the departed soul. When the party returns from the cremation ground, all wash themselves, and Karahprasad is distributed. Taking Karahprasad, which is normally a very joyous event, serves to declare that grief must end and normal life must return once more.

As soon as it can be conveniently arranged, the reading of the Guru Granth is begun by the family members. The bhog ceremony takes place on the tenth day with the *antam ardas* (the final ardas) recited on behalf of the deceased. Visitors wear white, black, and earth colors, more brilliant colors being reserved for weddings and other festive occasions. Thereafter, people continue to visit the family members of the dead person. They do not necessarily exchange words, but they sit in silence to share their grief and to commemorate their loss. Sikhs generally do not pay much attention to birthdays or wedding anniversaries, but death anniversaries of their loved ones are important. They continue to commemorate these occasions annually through bhog ceremonies. They keep the memory of the deceased alive by making gifts to the needy, to schools, libraries, and hospitals, and to the gurudwara itself. This final rite of passage is the most significant of them all, for it represents the ultimate stage on the path toward union with the Supreme Being.

CHAPTER 7

Sacred Space
and Sacred Time

A ccording to the Guru Granth, "Paradise is where the Ultimate Reality is praised." For Sikhs, wherever the Guru Granth is, that space is sacred. Whenever the Guru Granth is read, seen, remembered, or recited, that time is sacred. Certain days are more historically significant, however, and certain places have a value that comes from their association with the gurus or from their appeal to the senses.

The gurudwara, the Sikh place of worship, is, literally, a "door" (dwara) to ultimate enlightenment (guru). As much as possible, the gurudwara is designed to invite worshipers to feel the presence of the Transcendent Reality. It provides large areas of open space, so that people do not feel confined, and its outward appearance and size can vary. A gurudwara may be a single room in a private home; a simple, rustic structure in a small village; or a sumptuous, multistoried building, surrounded by a reflecting pool, in a large city. Any available hall or dwelling can be adapted, and people often meet in private homes.

One identifying mark of a gurudwara is the flag that flies over it. Even from a distance, the flag, which is yellow in color,

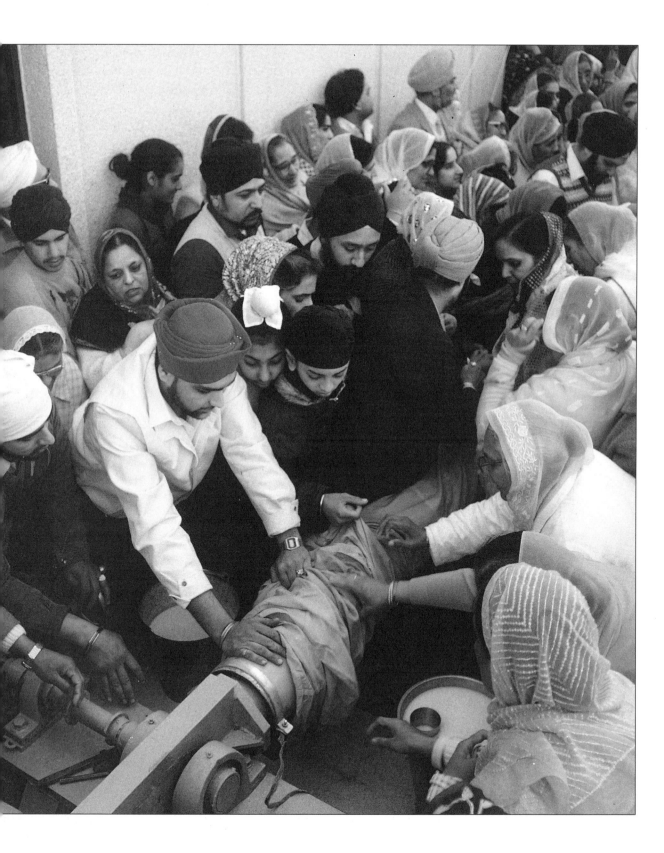

triangular in shape, and emblazoned with the emblem of the Sikh Khalsa, can be easily recognized. The emblem, a double-edged sword surrounded by two semicircular swords, can also be seen on the gurudwara's walls, windows, and doors.

A gurudwara has four doors, indicating welcome to people of all castes. Within, there is no altar or special holy place. The Guru Granth rests on a platform, the focus of attention. There are no statues or pictures that represent the Ultimate Reality in any form. The congregation can gather inside or outside the gurudwara—it does not really matter. There are no chairs or pews; all members sit on large mats spread on the floor. Women and men sit separately by tradition.

In India, a gurudwara can be easily recognized by its white domes and minarets, or towers, leading the eye toward the sky. A large courtyard within the gurudwara contributes to a feeling of openness. Many gurudwaras have a reflecting pool, and people bathe in its waters, sit near it to pray, or walk around it in contemplation. The gurudwaras in Asia are often modeled after the most sacred of all Sikh holy places, *Harimandir,* the Golden Temple, at Amritsar in India, and many are of historical note and are places of pilgrimage.

The Golden Temple

Harimandir, the Golden Temple, is the central shrine of the Sikhs. Sikh ritual and ceremony took form there. The temple is an example of the fundamental characteristics of Sikh art and architecture.

The Golden Temple rests on a platform in the middle of a sacred reflecting pool. Guru Ram Das originally built the pool in 1577, and named it Amritsar, or "pool of nectar." When Arjan succeeded to the guruship, he had the temple built in the sacred pool. Guru Arjan wanted this first Sikh shrine to be different from other places of worship. Thus, instead of ascending stairs, worshipers descend stairs to the Golden Temple, in humility. According to historical accounts, a Muslim, Miran Mir, laid the first foundation stone of the Sikh temple, once again reinforcing the Sikh principle that all faiths are different expressions of the One Ultimate Reality.

The reflecting pool lies like a peaceful oasis in the midst of the crowded, narrow streets of the city of Amritsar, which grew up around it. The pool is surrounded on four sides by a wide marble walkway, which in turn is enclosed by a white marble portico, or covered porch, several stories high, with a doorway on each side. The upper half of the building is covered in gold-plated copper sheets, giving the temple its name. At the southern side of the building are steps leading to the pool. Visitors descend the steps to obtain water from the pool. They might drink the water, sprinkle it on themselves, or fill bottles to take home to friends and relatives, especially the sick.

Both inside and out, the temple is covered with beautifully intricate carvings. The temple is never silent; sacred music plays twenty-two hours out of twenty-four. In the center of the ground

■ *Inside the historic Keshgarh Sahib temple, a leader preaches to the congregation during a service.*

Devotees dry off after immersion in the sacred pool at Amritsar, a source of physical and spiritual refreshment.

floor, the Guru Granth rests under a jewel-studded canopy, on silk and brocade cloth. From a second-floor balcony, granthis, or readers, take turns reading from the holy book. Before a reader ends his period of reading, the replacement reader steps in and the two granthis read a few words in unison. In this way, recitation of the holy word never stops. In addition, readings of the Guru Granth may be taking place on other levels of the temple at the same time.

The second story of the Golden Temple forms a sort of balcony with windows on either side. One set of windows looks outward toward the sacred pool and the town, while the other opens to the Guru Granth on the floor below. The ceilings and walls are inlaid with mirrors; every solid surface is decorated with delicate designs. The third floor consists of an open-air walkway. In the center is a small, square pavilion, topped by a golden dome. Visitors often pause to feed the birds that stop to rest there.

For Sikhs, the Golden Temple represents the highest attainment of beauty and tranquillity. Guru Arjan himself installed the Guru Granth there on August 16, 1604. When the Guru Granth was opened at random on that day, it revealed the following commandment:

> *Beautiful is this spot, beautiful is this pool filled*
>   *with ambrosial waters;*
> *Nectar flows, the wonderful task has been accomplished,*
>   *All desires have been fulfilled.*
> *Joy pervades the world, all suffering has ended.*

To Sikhs, the scriptural verse appropriately and auspiciously expresses the beauty of this sacred place at Amristar, the holiest shrine of the Sikhs.

The Five Takhts

In addition to the Golden Temple, the five *takhts*, or seats of temporal authority, are of major importance. In those places, Sikh leaders traditionally made decisions about the secular, or nonreligious, and religious aspects of Sikhism. The five seats are the *Akal Takht, Patna Sahib, Keshgarh Sahib, Hazur Sahib*, and *Damdama Sahib.* Several of these places are associated with Sikh history, especially with the life of the tenth guru, Gobind Singh.

The Akal Takht

The *Akal Takht,* or "Throne of the Formless," at Amritsar faces the Golden Temple. Sikhs regard it as the supreme seat of religious and temporal authority. Its foundation was originally laid in 1609 under the direction of Guru Hargobind. By that act, the sixth guru took community affairs out of the Golden Temple, reserving the temple for prayer and worship.

Guru Hargobind himself presided over important religious, social, and political gatherings at the Akal Takht. He held a court of justice, and many Sikhs went there to have their grievances heard and resolved. Over the centuries, additions expanded the Akal Takht into a five-story building with a golden dome and intricate interior decorations. This historic building was severely damaged in June 1984 when the Indian Army fired on Sikh separatists inside. It is still being restored.

Large numbers of Sikhs still assemble before the Akal Takht. The sound of a kettledrum announces the ceremonial activities that take place there. In the morning and the evening, the personal weapons of the Sikh gurus are displayed. The two most prized are the swords of Hargobind and Gobind Singh. Sikh leaders continue to proclaim formal Sikh policy from the halls of the takht. A saffron robe of honor conferred at the Akal Takht is a mark of great respect. It is given to those who render extraordinary service to the Sikh community.

Patna Sahib

The city of Patna is located five hundred miles east of Delhi, on the Ganges River. Both Guru Nanak and Siddhartha Gautama, Lord Buddha, the central figure of the Buddhist faith, are said to have visited there. Patna is also the birthplace of Gobind Singh, and a shrine there commemorates his birth. The shrine, in one of the old quarters of Patna, was originally the mansion of Salis Rai Johri, a follower of Guru Nanak. To show his devotion to the Sikh faith, he converted his home into an inn that was free for travelers and pilgrims. Guru Tegh Bahadur stayed there when he visited Patna. Later, a magnificent house was built above the inn. Eventually this building came to be known as the shrine *Takht Sri Harmandir Sahib.*

Gobind Singh, the son of Guru Tegh Bahadur, spent his early years in Patna, and many stories are told of his childhood there. One is about a queen named Mania, who was very sad because she had no children. She saw little Gobind, who was only four years old at the time, and she wished that she had a child of her own. The boy promised that he would be like a son to her. They became friends, and Mania gave him grain. Today, grain is still served in the langar at *Patna Sahib,* in recognition of the friendship between the boy Gobind and Queen Mania.

Relics of Guru Gobind Singh are preserved in this shrine. His sword, four arrows, and a pair of his sandals are displayed, along with some of his writings and those of his father, which are collected into a book.

Keshgarh Sahib

The town of Anandpur—literally the town of joy *(anand)*—is located in the foothills of the Himalayas, in the Shivalik valley of

■ *The Keshgarh Sahib at Anandpur in southern India marks the place where Guru Gobind Singh founded the Khalsa. Visitors to the shrine shop at a street market in its shadow.*

northwest India. There, *Takht Keshgarh Sahib* is a monument to the founding of the Khalsa by Guru Gobind Singh. The shrine is constructed at the place where the tenth guru administered *amrit,* or Sikh baptism, to his five beloved Sikhs. Each year, Sikhs reenact the founding of the Khalsa in Anandpur.

Other historically significant gurudwaras are located near Keshgarh Sahib. Gurudwara Guru ka Mahal, for instance, was build by the ninth guru, Tegh Bahadur, as his home. Guru Gobind

Singh's two sons, the grandsons of Tegh Bahadur, were born there. Guru Tegh Bahadur was beheaded under the Mogul rule in Delhi in 1675. Soon after, his follower Jaita carried the guru's head to Anandpur, where it was burned to ash, and the Gurudwara Sisganj (*sis* means "head") was built there to commemorate the event. The shrine in Delhi that marks the place of Guru Tegh Bahadur's martyrdom is also known as Gurudwara Sisganj.

Sri Hazur Sahib

Takht Sri Hazur Sahib in south central India is the site of the death of the tenth guru, Gobind Singh. It is located in Nanded, in the state of Maharashtra. Maharaja Ranjit Singh, a great Sikh leader, directed its construction between 1832 and 1837. It is a two-story gurudwara; both its architecture and its interior decoration are modeled after the Golden Temple. On the first floor, recitations from the Guru Granth take place continually, day and night.

The gurudwara's treasury contains several of Guru Gobind Singh's possessions. Besides jewelry and clothes, there are his golden dagger, two bows, a steel shield studded with precious stones, and five golden swords. The gurudwara also stables and cares for a horse that is said to be descended from the horse ridden by Guru Gobind Singh during his lifetime. The horse is led out for processions on special occasions. Throughout the year, thousands of Sikh devotees visit this historical shrine on the banks of the Godavari River.

Damdama Sahib

Damdama Sahib is situated near Bhatinda in the Punjab, just south of Amritsar. This gurudwara with its tranquil pool is sacred to the memory of Gobind Singh. The guru went there on the invitation of a devoted follower, Bhai Dalla, and liked the place so much that he stayed for more than nine months. His mirror, gun, and sword are displayed there.

At Damdama Sahib, Guru Gobind Singh pursued his literary work. There, Bhai Mani Singh prepared the final version of the Guru Granth under the tenth guru's direction. The gurudwara became known as a seat of Sikh learning. It was even called the Guru's Kashi, after a famous center for Sanskritic and Hindu studies.

On a pillar at Damdama Sahib are inscribed the words of Guru Gobind Singh expressing his firm faith in the Khalsa:

To the Khalsa belongs all
My home, my body, and all that I possess.

All Sikhs try to visit the five takhts at least once in their lifetime. Some make annual pilgrimages; others go only for special occasions. Some do not go to the takhts in person; instead, they have continuous readings *(akhandpaths)* recited on their behalf. They also send money for the readers, for the kitchen, and for silk coverings for the holy book.

Besides the Golden Temple and the five takhts, the Sikhs value many other gurudwaras. The birthplaces of the gurus and other sites also have special historical meaning. In the former princely state of Patiala, north of Delhi, two gurudwaras—Dukhniwaran Sahib in the city of Patiala and Bahadur Garh on its outskirts—are reminders of the ninth guru's visit. Sikhs travel there from all over the world. Visitors believe that a dip in the pool of Gurudwara Dukhniwaran Sahib will cure suffering—*dukhniwaran* literally means "the end of suffering *(dukh).*"

Similarly, the gurudwara in the old fort in Bhatinda stands at the place where Guru Gobind Singh won a battle against the Moguls. Moreover, it was at this fort that Empress Razia Sultana, the first woman ruler of India, was imprisoned before her execution. The gurudwara at the top of the fort is a small and simple one, but for Sikhs it is charged with historical significance.

Such sacred places bring the past to life for the Sikhs. Whenever they return to India, Sikhs from America, Europe, the Middle East, and the Far East try to visit their historical shrines with their children, passing on the tradition. These Sikh centers of faith and history continue to inspire the Sikhs spiritually, intellectually, and politically.

Sacred Times

Sikhs try to bring their faith into their lives at all times. They do not view one time as being more sacred than another. Long ago, Guru Nanak rejected the Indian custom of depending on astrology, the study of the heavenly bodies to determine "good" days. "We remain busy counting and determining auspicious days," he said, "but we do not know that the Ultimate Reality is above and beyond such considerations."

However, certain days of the month and of the year have an added element of festivity. The Sikhs inherited the ancient Indian lunar calendar based on the phases of the moon, so the new moon and the full moon are special for them. They incorporated the traditional Indian festivals into their year and gave them new meaning. They also added celebrations commemorating major events in Sikh history. Both the eternally returning seasons and the important and historic moments in Sikhism are celebrated with exuberance every year.

Sangrand and Masia

In Western countries, many Sikhs have adopted the custom of worshiping together on Sundays, but the opening, reading, and closing of the Guru Granth go on every day in people's homes and in the gurudwaras. Gurudwaras are open all the time, and people come and go as they wish. Sikhs do not have a weekly holy day equivalent to the Jewish or Christian sabbath. They do, however, regard the monthly sangrand and masia as special.

Sangrand is the first day of the month according to the Indian solar calendar. On this day, Sikhs may add hopes and wishes for the coming weeks to their daily prayers. Many who do not regularly go to the gurudwara do so on this occasion. They pray for prosperity, health, and peace throughout the month. In the village gurudwaras, warm Karahprasad replaces the sugar puffs more commonly used for the sacrament.

Masia is the darkest night of the month. Many Sikhs think it is an especially good time for bathing in the holy pool of the gurudwara. The pool at Dukhniwaran Sahib in Patiala, for instance, is usually filled with devotees from all over the region. This tradition began at Tarn Taran near Amritsar and continues to be observed with great festival spirit. Around ten at night, a procession carries the Guru Granth from the Akal Takht to the gurudwara in Tarn Taran. Sikh followers join in on the way, reciting hymns from the scripture. On route, people serve simple meals and sweet snacks. The procession reaches the shrine at Tarn Taran in the early hours of the morning, and everyone takes a dip

in the holy pool. Sikhs feel that sangrand and masia celebrations help them to stay in harmony with the natural rhythms of the month.

Baisakhi

Baisakhi is New Year's Day on the Indian calendar. It is the first day of Baisakh, a month that is approximately equivalent to the month of April. Hindus in India traditionally celebrated this day at Harwar, where two sacred rivers meet with a third, the holy Ganges. Guru Arjan began the Sikh tradition of Baisakhi celebrations at the Golden Temple. But even before that time, Sikhs assembled during the month of harvest to thank the Ultimate and listen to the teachings of their gurus. In 1699, Guru Gobind Singh created the Khalsa on Baisakhi Day. For Sikhs, this added special importance to the New Year celebration.

■ On **Baisakhi,** or New Year's Day, crowds of people from all over India gather outside the Golden Temple in Amritsar to celebrate at a fair that includes stalls of merchandise for sale, processions, musical performances, and religious observances.

Sikhs all over the world celebrate Baisakhi as a social, political, and religious occasion. The city of Amritsar, however, is a focal point in this annual event. Sikhs travel great distances to visit Harimandir, the Golden Temple, on this day. Singers and musicians perform throughout the day. The entire complex swarms with Sikh devotees bathing in the waters of the huge reflecting pool; listening to speakers and readers; preparing and consuming langar, the community meal that follows a service; making special offerings in the temple itself; and reverently circling the temple on the walkway as they contemplate and meditate.

The scene outside the Golden Temple complex is lively, as well. For the large farming element in India, Baisakhi is the last day to relax before the beginning of the harvest, so people make the most of it. They hold a large animal fair, at which they buy and sell goats, buffaloes, camels, and other livestock.

Sikhs also recall the Baisakhi festival of 1919. On that date, fearing conspiracy, the British rulers had forbidden the Sikhs to gather. But Sikhs did gather, in a small area near the Golden Temple called Jallian Wallah Bagh. The British fired on the Sikhs, and hundreds died. Today, political rallies take place at Jallian Wallah Bagh, where bullet holes from the massacre still scar the walls.

Important academic functions also take place on Baisakhi. New books are released, and scholars receive awards. The Khalsa community initiates new members on this birthday of the Khalsa itself. At gurudwaras, a new yellow Sikh flag replaces the old one. Overall, New Year's Day is regarded as a good time for all kinds of new beginnings.

Divali

Around the time of Christmas and Hanukkah in the West, people in India celebrate *Divali. Divali* is a shortened form of the word *deepavali,* which literally means "a string of lights." For Hindus it is a major festival, welcoming the visit of the Lakshmi, the goddess of wealth and prosperity. It also commemorates the return of King Rama and Queen Sita to their kingdom of Ayodhya after fourteen years of exile. In Sikhism, however, it is a reminder of the time when their sixth guru returned to Amritsar after the Mogul rulers released him from the fort of Gwalior.

smeared with yellows, greens, reds, and blues. The scene in parks, streets, and shopping districts is one of vibrant color and merry-making.

Guru Gobind Singh gave this traditional spring festival a Sikh character. In Anandpur, he initiated the *Hola Mohalla*, a three-day festival during which Sikhs trained as soldiers. Although held at the same time as Holi, Hola Mohalla had a more serious purpose. What took place were contests in horsemanship, wrestling, and archery as well as mock battles and military exercises. The guru also encouraged competitions in music and poetry. Sikhs still celebrate the festival annually at Anandpur. They hold a large fair with singing, discussions, and athletic competitions.

Basant

Yet another spring festival is *Basant*, which simply means "spring." During the time when the yellow mustard blooms in the Punjabi fields, people wear yellow and eat yellow rice. In the villages of India, the rooftops are full of youngsters flying kites. There are competitions to see whose kite will fly highest, but part of the fun is to sabotage other kites. The children attach bits of glass to their kites and try to cut their opponents' kite strings by flying across them. Basant is a colorful and festive time.

Rakhri

The festival of *Rakhri* comes in mid-August. A *rakhri* is a bright band that a sister ties around her brother's right wrist as she puts candy in his mouth. In turn, the brother gives his sister a gift of money, clothes, or jewelry. This brief ritual symbolizes the bond between brother and sister. The sister prays for the long life and prosperity of her brother, and the brother promises to help and protect his sister whether she is single or married. Many Sikh families say ardas, the basic prayer in which Sikhs remember their ten gurus and the Guru Granth, before the tying of the rakhri. They may distribute karaprasad afterward.

Gurpurabs

Gurpurabs are Sikh anniversaries. The birth dates of gurus, important historical events, and the martyrdom of Sikh heroes are remembered annually. After the new year begins in April, the first event in the Sikh calendar is the martyrdom of Guru Arjan. This falls in the month of *Jaith*, which corresponds to May-June on

■ The Festivals of Sikhism

April 13	Baisakhi
April	Birthday of Guru Tegh Bahadur
	Birthday of Guru Arjan
May	Birthday of Guru Angad
	Birthday of Guru Amar Das
May/June	Martydom of Guru Amar Arjan
June	Birthday of Guru Hargobind
July	Birthday of Guru Har Krishan
October/November	Divali
November	Birthday of Guru Nanak
November/December	Martyrdom of Guru Tegh Bahadur
December/January	Birthday of Guru Gobind Singh
March	Hola Mohalla

the Western calendar. In August, Sikhs celebrate the installation of the Guru Granth in the Golden Temple. As winter comes and Divali approaches, Sikhs celebrate the birthdays of the first and the tenth gurus, only a month apart. Guru Nanak's birthday falls in November. It is clebrated as the origin of the Sikh faith. This event is followed by Guru Gobind Singh's birthday in December. The martyrdom of the tenth guru's young sons also falls during December. It is preceded by the day of the martyrdom of Guru Tegh Bahadur.

During the various gurpurabs, a float decorated with flowers carries the Guru Granth in a procession through the city or village. Sikhs recite scriptural hymns and serve langar. Wherever the procession goes, people come out of their homes to see it. They cover their heads and remove their shoes to show homage to the holy book.

To commemorate gurpurabs, people gather in the gurudwaras. Sikh scholars deliver lectures, and uninterrupted readings of the Guru Granth take place, followed by bhog ceremonies, in which worshipers say prayers and receive Karahprasad. People also enjoy exhibits of Sikh treasures at shrines like the Golden Temple.

 American Sikhs and non-Sikhs join to celebrate Peace Prayer Day, a cultural event dedicated to creating peace with the earth, within themselves, and with one another.

Sikhs in places such as Toronto, San Francisco, New York, and Washington, D.C., celebrate these occasions as well. Often they combine religious ceremonies with intellectual and cultural events. They invite musicians and lecturers from India and hold lavish langars and celebrations. They present seminars organized around Sikh themes in which both Sikhs and non-Sikhs may participate. They may organize plays, poetry readings, and performances of folk music from their heritage.

Special customs are related to certain gurpurabs. Sikhs serve cold milk in water, a welcome refreshment in a hot month, on the anniversary of Guru Arjan's martyrdom. Arjan was tortured to death by being dipped in hot oil and sand and then thrown into cold waters. Sikhs also recall the martyrdom of Guru Gobind Singh's young sons in a special way. Zorowar Singh and Fateh

Singh were bricked up behind a wall by rulers who wanted them to convert to Islam. The two boys held to their Sikh faith and died heroes. Millions gather each December in the Sirhind area of the Punjab to honor their memory. Farmers bring out wheat, grain, milk, and vegetables, and everyone shares enthusiastically in preparing and enjoying langar.

These festivals enable Sikhs to share in their heritage and keep the foundations of the community strong and lively. Such occasions help to deepen and enrich the Sikh experience, whether participants celebrate them by praying in a gurudwara or by simply participating in the festival atmosphere. For the Sikhs, sacred space and sacred time are not two different or separate things. Rather they merge into the singular experience of the sacred that is beyond all space and time.

CHAPTER 8

Women
and Sikhism

*F*rom the beginning of Sikh tradition, women have held an important place. Sikh history holds stories of the many women who helped in many ways to shape the faith. Women have been active and central subjects in Sikh history, and they are remembered in prayer and song along with their male counterparts.

Until Guru Nanak's time, women in Indian society had long played a subordinate role. The inferior status of women, however, did not fit into the guru's vision of total equality for all people under the Universal Reality. Nanak declared:

> *Of woman are we born, of woman conceived,*
> *To woman engaged, to woman married.*
> *Woman we befriend, by woman do civilizations continue.*
> *When a woman dies, a woman is sought for.*
> *It is through woman that order is maintained.*
> *Then why call her inferior from whom all great ones are born?*

The early gurus repudiated Indian customs that denied women an equal place in society. They spoke out against the Hindu custom of *sati*, in which a widow had to sacrifice her own

Preceding page-
Sikh women, their heads
covered in reverence,
listen to the sacred word
at a worship service. By
tradition, women and
men sit separately in
the gurudwara.

life at her husband's cremation. They dismissed the Islamic practice of *purdah*, whereby women had to veil their faces and bodies in public. And they rejected the custom of female infanticide, in which newborn girls, thought to be less valuable than boys, were put to death.

In some traditions, women are regarded as "polluted," or unclean, for a part of each month and after childbirth. They may be barred from religious services during these times and required to undergo ritual cleansing before they can participate again. In Sikhism, however, women's bodies are considered whole and strong because of their function in giving birth. Women are the equal of men.

The Ultimate Reality of Sikhism includes male and female alike. The Guru Granth affirms: "It itself is man; It itself is woman." The Sikh gurus expressed the Ultimate in feminine imagery. To identify the spark of Ultimate Reality within everyone, the gurus used the feminine noun Joti, meaning "light." The insubstantial image of light helps to make both male and female Sikhs aware of the Ultimate within themselves.

Women in the Sikh Community

There is no priesthood in Sikhism. To lead in worship, Sikhs choose people from within their sangat, or congregation. These leaders may be either women or men, as Sikhs consider members of both sexes equally endowed with moral and spiritual faculties. Both men and women can read the Guru Granth. Both can recite kirtan, the sacred hymns. Both can officiate at any ceremony.

The third guru, Amar Das, established procedures that would ensure the participation of men and women in organizing and administering Sikh communities. In some branches of Sikhism, the custom of turning to a guru for spiritual guidance has survived, but in general, Sikhs make their own spiritual journeys, guided by the Guru Granth.

Women in Sikh History

Although little is known about the women in Guru Nanak's life—his sister Nanaki, his mother Tripta, and his wife Sulakhni—many Sikhs believe that Nanak's message regarding equality of

*Three Sikh women stir yogurt for **langar**, the community meal.*

the sexes and his rejection of customs that were harmful to women were signs of their influence on him. Of special importance was Nanaki. She was five years older than Nanak, and the boy was named for her. Many clues suggest that she and her brother were very close. When Nanaki married and left home, her brother went to live with her and her new family. She was the first to recognize his special gifts, and when others thought that Nanak had drowned in the River Bein, Nanaki remained convinced that he was an immortal soul.

Other Sikh women, too, have been important to the Sikh faith. A few are described below.

Mata Khivi was the wife of Angad, the second guru. The Guru Granth praises her warmth and generosity. Sikhs remember this outgoing woman, who died in 1582, for the feelings of affection and hospitality that she brought to the institution of langar. Under her liberal direction, it became not just a symbolic meal, but a real feast, with Mata Khivi supplying a delicious rice pudding. For her contributions to the tradition of langar, Mata Khivi is described in the Guru Granth as "a thickly leafed tree" that brings shade and comfort to weary travelers. Sikhs also remember her as a wise advisor to her sons on spiritual and social matters.

Bibi Bhani was the daughter of the third guru, Amar Das. She later married her father's successor, Guru Ram Das, and became the mother of Guru Arjan, the fifth guru, who compiled the Guru Granth. Sikhs remember Bibi Bhani as a strong woman with immense moral fervor. As the daughter, wife, and mother of gurus, she had a profound influence. Guru Arjan's poetry contains a wealth of feminine images as if to underscore the importance of his mother's voice in his life. Bibi Bhani died in Taran Taran in 1598. In her memory, Guru Arjan had a well built that provided water for refreshment and for agriculture, a fitting monument to her life.

Mai Bhago was a courageous woman from the Amritsar district. During wartime, when a long siege had brought hardship in Anandpur, she rallied people who had fled that town and led them back to fight for Guru Gobind Singh. She herself took part in the battle at Muktsar on December 19, 1705, where she displayed courage and skill. Mai Bhago died in 1708. A monument to her memory stands at Hazur Sahib. The Sikh poet Bhai Vir Singh calls her a beacon of progress, a luminous star that provides light to all.

When Guru Gobind Singh stirred the water of the first Khalsa initiation ceremony with his sword, his wife, *Mata Sahib Kaur*, added the sugar to the steel bowl. It was she who brought an element of celestial sweetness to the ritual. From that day on, Khalsa members have traced their historical and spiritual beginnings to Guru Gobind Singh and Mata Sahib Kaur. The Khalsa members declare themselves to be the direct descendants of these two spiritual parents, who are equally important in the Khalsa family. Mata Sahib Kaur died in 1735.

Mata Gujri was born in 1627 and became the wife of Guru Tegh Bahadur. She was imprisoned in Sirhind with her two younger grandchildren, and all three died there as martyrs to the Sikh faith. Sikhs remember her especially for strengthening the faith of the young boys, who were sealed alive behind a brick wall and chose to die there rather than renounce Sikhism. The shrine of Joti Saroop marks the site where Mata Gujri was cremated on December 28, 1704. Her husband and two other grandsons also died as martyrs for the Sikh faith.

Sada Kaur was the mother-in-law of Maharaja Ranjit Singh, the first Sikh emperor. When he assumed the throne, he was only nineteen, and he turned to his mother-in-law, whose counsel enabled him to unify the Punjab and create a Sikh state. A passionate patriot, Sada Kaur possessed great courage on the battlefield. The best part of her triumph, however, lay in peaceful victory. Under her direction and guidance, Ranjit Singh was able to take control of the capital at Lahore without bloodshed. Sada Kaur also funded and administered Sikh institutions of learning. She died in Amritsar in 1832.

Maharani Jindan was born in 1817. She was married to Maharaja Ranjit Singh in 1835, toward the end of his life, and bore him a son, Dilip Singh, in 1837. The Maharaja died in 1839 and four years later, six-year-old Dilip Singh succeeded him as leader of the Sikhs in the Punjab. Jindan, Dilip Singh's mother, became regent, or caretaker ruler of the Sikh empire. Maharani Jindan was famous for her keen intelligence. The British, then in power in India, found her a constant threat. Following an uprising in which the British put down the Khalsa, Jindan was accused of conspiracy and imprisoned. Her young son was taken to England and converted to Christianity. The Maharani continued to write powerful letters from prison. She later went to England and convinced her son to return to Sikhism. She died in England on August 1, 1863.

Women and Sikh Literature

Sikh literature also contains women characters who display physical, intellectual, and spiritual strength. Two fictional heroines have been special favorites among the Sikh reading public—

Sundari and Rani Raj Kaur, the creations of Bhai Vir Singh (1873–1957) a Sikh scholar, poet, and novelist.

Sundari, first published about a hundred years ago, is the first novel in the Punjabi language and still the most widely read of all Sikh popular literature. Bhai Vir Singh began to write this novel when he was a young man—a student in high school. In this fast-paced adventure, the young woman who is the main character is kidnapped by the Moguls, the Sikhs' traditional enemies. Rescued by a brother who has become a Sikh, she joins the Khalsa and takes the name Sundari. Within the Khalsa, she lives according to the teachings of the guru and embodies the Sikh ideal. The story of Sundari, with its vigorous action and high principles, captured the Sikh imagination as no other work of fiction ever had. Generations of Punjabi readers have been touched by Sundari's qualities of dedication, daring, and charity. The book has inspired many people to be initiated into the Khalsa.

Another of Bhai Vir Singh's works, *Rana Surat Singh,* published in 1905, gave Sikhs a second great fictional heroine. The five stages of spiritual ascension enumerated in the Jap, the first prayer of the Guru Granth, provide the framework for the book. In this epic, the heroine, Rani Raj Kaur, makes a journey of faith, eventually realizing the highest stage of spiritual awareness. At the same time, she moves in her daily life from a state of weakness and inaction to one of full participation in affairs of the world. Her spiritual experience gives her a new sense of self and a new orientation in the world, completely changing her domestic, social, and political life. At the end of the book, Rani Raj Kaur assumes the political duties of her state and presides as a strong and wise ruler.

From Rani Raj Kaur's story, Sikhs take the message that the Sikh spiritual experience—the love for Ultimate Reality and the ascent into the sacred—is grounded in the love of fellow beings. The intimate relationships of the world—mother and daughter, sister and sister, husband and wife—are essential to the human condition. These relationships exist through the relationship of humans to the Ultimate Reality. For Sikhs, the spiritual ascent has practical results. It helps them to recognize the fundamental unity of people and the universe.

The role of women in the Sikh community, feminine images in Sikh scripture, stories of women in Sikh history, and female models in Sikh fiction all provide insights into the ways in which women enrich and expand human life. Each in its own way helps to bridge the gap between the sacred and the secular.

■ Sikh women in India use ashes to clean the stainless steel langar pots before washing them. Cleaning utensils in this way is considered to be a special act of **seva,** or service to the community.

CHAPTER 9

Sikh Tradition
and Modern Culture

ooner or later, every religious tradition comes
into contact with the demands of modern life. If a religion is to
remain alive, it must be able to meet the needs and demands of
contemporary people. Sikhism has always encouraged its followers to participate fully in the political, social, and cultural climate
in which they live. For this reason, it has been successful in blend-
ing tradition and modern life.

A Modernizing Traditionalist:
Maharaja Ranjit Singh

After the death of Guru Gobind Singh in 1708, the leadership of the Sikhs fell to the Khalsa under Banda Singh Bahadur.
Bahadur resisted the Mogul rulers until 1716, when he was captured and executed. The Khalsa withdrew to the hills and remained there for several years in small bands.

In 1738, Persian and then Afghan invasions began to weaken
the Mogul rule. Organized groups of the Khalsa reappeared and,
in 1761, established themselves once again as rulers in the Punjab.
These groups struggled among themselves for power, however,
and political life in the Punjab was far from stable.

In 1799, a new leader emerged. Guided by Sada Kaur, his mother-in-law, Ranjit Singh, the nineteen-year-old leader of a Khalsa band, seized power peacefully in the city of Lahore. Over the next two years, he carefully consolidated his strength, integrating twelve warring Sikh bands into a sovereign state. On the day of Baisakhi, 1801, the Sikhs crowned him maharajah, or ruling prince, of the Punjab. He ruled for forty years and is known as the Lion of the Punjab. The British had taken over much of India, but Ranjit Singh's rule was strong and steady, and the British did not challenge him.

Maharaja Ranjit Singh was a striking figure. Dressed always in white, he habitually wore on his arm the Koh-i-noor diamond, at the time the largest and most valuable gem in the world and now one of the British Crown Jewels. He had lost an eye early in life, and his one-eyed stare was penetrating. Under his rule, new gurudwaras were built and many old ones renovated. He strictly enforced Sikh rules, demanding that even foreigners in his court refrain from cutting their hair and beards, eating beef, or smoking tobacco in public.

However, the maharaja was open to new ideas. He welcomed people from Europe and America to his court and questioned them closely to discover modern ways that he could bring to the Punjab. He hired French, Italian, British, American, and Russian military experts to train and instruct the Khalsa, which became one of the finest fighting forces in the world. The surgeon general of the Khalsa was French, one of its engineers was a Spaniard, and a gunnery instructor, Alexander Gardner, was born in Wisconsin.

Visitors came from all parts of the world to the maharaja's cosmopolitan court. The German scientist Charles Hugel wrote that the Punjab under Ranjit Singh was safer than territories ruled by the British. Another visitor, Joseph Wolff, an English missionary, told of his surprise on hearing someone in the palace singing "Yankee Doodle." It was Josiah Harlan, a native of Philadelphia, and governor of one of the maharaja's provinces. In 1834, the American missionary John C. Lowrie compared Amritsar to two of the world's most famous cities, calling it "the Sikh Athens and Jerusalem."

Besides being known as an excellent host, the maharaja was recognized as a fine diplomat. The British called on him regularly to intercede for them with other Indian princes. Under his reign, the first dictionary and grammar of the Punjabi language were printed, and Punjabi translations of portions of the Christian Bible appeared for the first time. From the beginning, he respected all cultures. When he was crowned by a Sikh descendant of Guru Nanak, Hindus gathered in their temples and Muslims, in their mosques to pray for his long life.

■ *A shrine in Lahore City, Pakistan, memorializes Maharaja Ranjit Singh.*

The Decline of the Sikh State

Ranjit Singh's death in 1839 created a power struggle. His eldest son, Kharak Singh, a weak leader, was quickly deposed by his own son, Naunihal Singh, who died soon after in an accident.

Naunihal's mother, Chand Kaur, seized power, only to lose it after a few months to Sher Singh, Ranjit Singh's second son. Sher Singh had Chand Kaur killed, setting off a period of violent retaliation and counter-retaliation. After two years, Ranjit Singh's last surviving son, Dilip Singh, only six years old, was named maharaja under the guidance of his mother, Jindan.

In 1845, with Sikh leadership severely weakened, the British set out to take control of the Punjab. The Khalsa moved to stop them. After nearly a year of bitter fighting known as the First Sikh War, the British defeated the Khalsa. They left the Sikh government in place but installed a British governor and banished Jindan.

In 1849, the Sikhs rose up against the British a second time in what is called the Second Sikh War. Defeated once again, the Khalsa surrendered. This time, the British took complete command, removing the young maharaja to England and establishing British rule in the Punjab. Under British domination, Sikh morale reached a low ebb. Many Sikhs gave up Sikh practices and adopted those of their new rulers. By the census of 1868, the Sikhs, roughly estimated at about ten million in Maharaja Ranjit Singh's time, dwindled to just over a million.

The Singh Sabha and Bhai Vir Singh

In 1873, the Singh Sabha, a movement of reform and renewal, arose. Begun in Amritsar by three eminent Sikhs, it aimed at recapturing the original message of the early gurus and recovering the Sikh identity. Although it looked to the past to revive the original purity of belief, it also looked to the future with a view to leading the community into the modern age.

Bhai Vir Singh was only one year old when the Singh Sabha began. As the son of one of its founders, he grew up close to the movement. He became its most eloquent spokesperson. A gifted writer, Bhai Vir Singh interpreted the significance of the Sikh tradition to the next generation and helped to bring about Sikh revival.

Bhai Vir Singh received a Western education. He studied English literature and history, and used his studies to appraise his own Sikh heritage in a modern light. Writing in the Punjabi language, he introduced a wide variety of literary genres into the culture. He wrote in almost every form—poetry, fiction, essays, newspaper articles, and scholarly works on Sikhism. His work marks the beginning of a renaissance in Sikh culture. His fiction, particularly, including the classic *Sundari,* helped to explain the goals of Sikhism and how they might be carried out in everyday life. In Bhai Vir Singh's work, tradition and the modern world intersect.

Sikhism Today

Until the middle of the twentieth century, India was the colonial state of an imperial power, a situation that limited the opportunities for the exchange of ideas between East and West. Indian independence after World War II created the world's largest democracy and the second largest secular state (after China) and brought a major new player onto the world stage.

The young Indian nation has not been without its problems. Creating a federal India required uniting hundreds of factions representing different religions, racial and ethnic groups, and languages. For the Sikhs, Indian independence brought many changes, not all of them welcome. Under the British, whose policies they supported, the Sikhs had enjoyed a favored position. With Indian independence, they lost that advantage. Many Sikhs were uprooted when a part of their homeland was partitioned into Pakistan. The Hindu majority in New Delhi, the Indian capital, tended to rule inflexibly with regard to the Sikhs. Even more distressing to a proud people, the Sikh religion was not recognized in the Indian Constitution, although Hinduism, Islam, and Christianity were.

These and other conditions bred Sikh dissatisfaction with the government and created pressure for home rule in the Punjab, the Sikh homeland. The Punjab is important to India, both economically—perhaps eighty percent of India's agricultural produce comes from the Punjab—and defensively, with both Russia and China lying near its northern border. Most Indian administrations reacted harshly to Sikh requests for greater control of the region.

Sikhs tend to be prosperous and visible in India, making up a sizable portion of professional and business people. However,

Sikhs represent only two percent of the population. Only in the Punjab do they hold a majority, and that a small one. By numbers alone, they could not muster the political strength necessary to gain their political ends. Indeed, Sikh prosperity may have worked against them, fueling both the Sikh perception that they deserved more political power and autonomy and the perception of the Hindu majority that they already had enough. Government repression encouraged the growth of a militant right-wing faction of Sikhs for whom the only goal was separation from India.

Under Prime Minister Indira Gandhi, matters deteriorated steadily. Although Sikhs had had their own government in the Punjab since 1966, the Gandhi government suspended elections there after 1980, and in 1983 dismantled the state government, administering the affairs of the Punjab from the Indian capital in New Delhi. Thousands of Sikhs were imprisoned and held on nothing more than suspicion. The conflict between Sikh separatists and government troops became increasingly violent.

In 1984, the Indian army fired on a band of separatists who had made the area around the Golden Temple their headquarters. In addition to separatists, as many as a thousand ordinary worshipers were killed. Most people had not supported the separatists, but the deaths and the destruction of temple buildings caused widespread anguish. A short time later, Gandhi was assassinated by two of her own bodyguards, who were Sikhs. The Sikh-Hindu antagonism was greatly intensified.

Indira Gandhi's successor, her son Rajiv Gandhi, recognized that the separatists represented only a small part of the total Sikh population. He tried to defuse an explosive situation by signing an agreement with Sikh moderates, promising to restore elections, to give Sikhs more economic and political power, and to recognize the Sikh religion officially. Sikh separatists saw the agreement with the Indian government as a betrayal. The official who signed the agreement was assassinated, leaving the main political party leaderless. The Indian government later failed to carry out some of the terms of the agreement, action that further weakened both the government's credibility and that of the Sikh moderates. In 1987 and 1988, the condition worsened. Thousands of people died in the Punjab, mainly in skirmishes between the

government and militants or suspected militants, but also in attacks that cost the lives of many Hindus and moderate Sikhs.

Many Sikhs in the Punjab feel that the policies of the Indian government have led to a level of violence that threatens the very existence of their faith. The historic harmony between Hindus and Sikhs that Guru Nanak proclaimed and for which Guru Tegh Bahadur died has been shattered, and the Sikhs themselves have been divided, with Sikhs attacking Sikhs. Recently, leaders have called for an end to violence among the various Sikh factions, but the political situation remains unresolved.

India's political problems primarily affect the Sikhs in India. There are Sikhs all over the world, but outside India, Sikhs face

■ *During elections in the Punjab in 1992, a Sikh volunteer receives orders to guard a polling place threatened by the conflict between moderates and separatists.*

other problems. They may suffer discrimination because they are considered to be people of color, because little is known about their religion, and because their customs and manner of dress set them apart.

In spite of such difficulties, however, there are many signs that Sikhism is healthy and strong. Sikhs' emphasis on fellowship has enabled them to establish vibrant, supportive religious communities wherever they have settled in the Middle East, Europe, Britain, Canada, and the United States, and to practice their faith with enthusiasm and pride. In their new homes, Sikhs generally win respect because of their strong work ethic and value system.

The emergence of India into the world scene fostered an attitude of equality, mutual respect, and genuine interest between East and West that has helped to create free dialogue between these two cultures. As the West has gained wider experience with and knowledge of the East, its interest in all Eastern religions, including Sikhism, has grown.

The quincentennial in 1969 of the birth of Guru Nanak and the three hundredth anniversary in 1966 of the birth of Guru Gobind Singh generated broad interest in Sikhism. Research grants and endowments to colleges and universities in various parts of

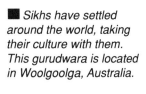
Sikhs have settled around the world, taking their culture with them. This gurudwara is located in Woolgoolga, Australia.

the world spurred academic research. Indian universities created departments especially devoted to Sikh studies. These institutions have produced a large body of scholarly literature on Sikhism that is now available to scholars in both the East and the West.

The five-hundred-year-old Sikh tradition harmonizes well with the modern world. Guru Nanak's message is that people must ignore external appearances and recognize the divine spark of Ultimate Reality in others and in the world around us. It is an ideal of diversity. Diversity, however, is not merely studying, working, and traveling with people of different complexions, languages, religions, and ways of dressing. Rather it means an active engagement with others. It involves three steps: knowing the other, knowing oneself, and communicating with one another at a deep level of friendship.

Sikh philosophy offers an inner spiritual way to that infinite One. Followers see that way as liberating. Sikh ethics requires people to live more fully in this world by helping their neighbors. Sikhism offers a heightened awareness of connection with other people, with the natural rhythms of nature, and with the past. It is an experience of exuberance and joy in the modern world's tightly scheduled routine.

Sikhs see the message of Guru Nanak as a response to contemporary problems of racism, gender, and class. The specific identity of the Sikhs and the particular religion of Sikhism present a Universal Reality that can be experienced by people of all races and creeds. The Sikh ideal of unity in diversity offers a hopeful direction for the world of the future.

CHAPTER NOTES

page 18   "Both Hindus and Muslims will venerate him. . . ." from the *Janamsakhis*.

page 18   "If a Hindu saw him, he would exclaim: . . . " from the *Janamsakhis*.

page 19   "Let compassion be your cotton; . . ." from the *Puratan Janamsakhi*.

page 21   "As the Almighty willed, Nanak the devotee was . . ." from the *Janamsakhis*.

page 37   "My sword today wants a head . . ."
page 38   "I wish you all to embrace one creed and . . ."
           Sujan Rai Bhandari Batalia, *Khulasat-ut-Tawarikh*, quoted in
           Kapur Singh, *The Baisakhi of Guru Gobind Singh*.

page 42   "On the platter lie arranged three delicacies: . . ." from the *Mundavani*.

page 48   *Ikk Oan Kar*—There is one Being . . ." from the *Mul Mantra*.

page 49   ". . . Hindus and Muslims are one! . . ." from the Guru Granth.

page 55   "There is a light in all and the light is That One. . . ." from the
           Guru Granth.
           "In Nature It is seen, in nature heard, . . ." from the Guru Granth.
           "You are the Primal Being, you are the Infinite Creator . . ."
           from the Guru Granth.

page 59   "Those who hear, appropriate and nurture love in their hearts, . . ."
           from the Guru Granth.
           "They who worship the One with adoring love . . ." from the
           Guru Granth.

page 75   "I present this child and with Your Grace . . ." Sir Jogendra
           Singh, *Sikh Ceremonies*.

page 84   "Wake up my mind, wake up from the oblivion of sleep . . ."
           from the Guru Granth.
           "The day of my wedding is fixed, . . ." from the *Kirtan Sohila*.

page 91   "Beautiful is this spot, beautiful is this pool . . ." from the Guru
           Granth.

page 95   "To the Khalsa belongs all . . ." Words of Guru Gobind Singh,
           inscribed at Takht Damdama Sahib.

page 104   "Of woman are we born, of woman conceived, . . ." from the
           Guru Granth.

GLOSSARY

Amrit—Nectar of immortality.

Anand Karaj—Literally, "blissful occasion." The Sikh marriage ceremony, constituting both religious and legal aspects of the marriage.

Ardas—The prayer that forms the culmination of the Sikh service.

Baisakhi—The Sikh New Year's Day, a festival that takes place in April and celebrates the founding of the Khalsa.

Dharam—Moral duty; the first stage of spiritual ascension as recorded in the Jap.

Divali—The Festival of Lights, celebrated in October or November.

Granthis—Readers of the Guru Granth during Sikh worship.

Gurpurabs—Anniversary celebrations commemorating Gurus' birth dates, the martyrdom of Sikhs, and historical events.

Guru Granth—In Sikhism, the sacred text that contains the compositions of the Sikh gurus, as well as those of Hindu and Muslim saints, and forms the center of all Sikh ceremony and ritual; also known as **Adi Granth**, literally "first book," a title given to the Guru Granth.

Gurudwara—Literally, "door to enlightenment." The Sikh place of worship.

Gyan—Literally, "knowledge." The second stage of spiritual ascension as recorded in the Jap.

Harimandir—The House of the Divine Being. Harimandir is the central shrine of the Sikhs, built by Arjan, the fifth guru, and located in Amritsar, India. Because its exterior appears to be covered with gold, it is called the Golden Temple.

Jap—The morning prayer of the Sikhs. The Jap forms the beginning of the Guru Granth and presents the foundation of Sikh philosophy and doctrine.

Karahprasad—The Sikh sacrament. Made of equal amounts of flour, sugar, water, and butter, this sweet mixture is placed in the cupped palms of the members of the congregation at the end of the Sikh service.

Kaur—Literally, "princess." The surname given to all Sikh women.

Khalsa—Literally, "pure ones." The fellowship of Sikhs founded by Gobind Singh, the tenth guru, on Baisakhi in 1699.

Khanda—The double-edged sword used as a symbol of Sikhism.

Kirtan—The singing of hymns, an important part of Sikh service. Verses from the Guru Granth are sung in the appropriate musical measures, often accompanied by such instruments as the harmonium and the tabla (drums).

Langar—The community kitchen. In Sikh shrines and during Sikh gatherings, men and women cook meals and, sitting in rows on the floor, eat together, regardless of race and caste.

Mul Mantra—The short passage that begins the Guru Granth; Sikhism's essential creed describing the Oneness of Reality and Its transcendent nature.

Panj Pyare—Literally, the "five beloved." The name given to the five Sikhs who were prepared to give their life for their faith; the first five members of the Khalsa.

Punjab—The fertile farming region in northwest India that is home to the Sikhs; literally, "five rivers" because of its relationship to the Indus River and its five tributaries.

Sangat—Gathering or congretation.

Sat Sri Akal—Literally, "Truth is the Timeless One." The Sikh greeting, said while pressing one's palms together and gently bowing.

Singh—Literally, "lion-hearted." The surname of all Sikh men, first used by Guru Gobind Singh to eliminate caste distinctions and to instill heroism in his people.

Wahe Guru—Literally, "Wonderful Guru." The expression is equivalent to saying, "Amen," "Cheers," "Bon Appetit," and "God Bless You," and it is announced before and after any major or minor undertaking.

FOR FURTHER READING

Cole, W. Owen, and Piara Singh Sambhi. *The Sikhs: Their Religious Beliefs and Practices.* London: Routledge and Kegan Paul, Ltd., 1978.

McLeod, W. H., ed. and trans. *Textual Sources for the Study of Sikhism.* Tottawa, N.J.: Barnes and Noble Books, 1984.

———. *The Sikhs: History, Religion and Society.* New York: Columbia University Press, 1989.

Singh, Daljit, and Angela Smith. *The Sikh World.* London: Macdonald & Company, 1985.

Singh, Harbans. *Mahindi and Other Stories.* Delhi: Navyug Publishers, 1984.

———. *The Heritage of the Sikhs.* Delhi: Manohar Publishers, 1983.

Singh, Patwant. *The Golden Temple.* Hong Kong: ET Publishing, Ltd., 1988.

INDEX